I Am Simple Natural Life

Your Guide to Taking Practical Steps to Lead a More Natural Life

SARAH BROOKS

Copyright © 2020 Sarah Brooks

I Am Simple Natural Life

No part of this publication may be reproduced, distributed, or transmitted in any form or by any means, including photocopying, recording, or other electronic or mechanical methods, without the prior written permission of the publisher, except in the case of brief quotations embodied in critical reviews and certain other non-commercial uses permitted by copyright law.

Although the author and publisher have made every effort to ensure that the information in this book was correct at press time, the author and publisher do not assume and hereby disclaim any liability to any party for any loss, damage, or disruption caused by errors or omissions, whether such errors or omissions result from negligence, accident, or any other cause.

Adherence to all applicable laws and regulations, including international, federal, state, and local governing professional licensing, business practices, advertising, and all other aspects of doing business in the UK, US, Canada, or any other jurisdiction is the sole responsibility of the reader and consumer.

Neither the author nor the publisher assumes any responsibility or liability whatsoever on behalf of the consumer or reader of this material. Any perceived slight of any individual or organization is purely unintentional.

The resources in this book are provided for informational purposes only and should not be used to replace the specialized training and professional judgment of a healthcare or mental healthcare professional.

Neither the author nor the publisher can be held responsible for the use of the information provided within this book. Please always consult a trained professional before making any decision regarding treatment of yourself or others.

All rights reserved.

ISBN: 978-1-8381982-1-3

This book is dedicated to Enid, Emily, Alice, and Florence.
You are my inspiration to be my best version of me.

I Am Simple Natural Life

CONTENTS

Introduction	Pg 1
Section One: Household	Pg 7
Section Two: Lifestyle	Pg 43
Section Three: Well-Being	Pg 89
Conclusion	Pg 129
Acknowledgements	Pg 132
About the Author	Pg 133
Feedback	Pg 134

I Am Simple Natural Life

FREE DOWNLOAD FOR READERS

In 'I Am Simple Natural Life' I provide lots of practical tips and suggestions for ways you can make changes to lead a more naturally aligned life.

However, I know that sometimes it can be hard to know exactly where to start, so I have created a Kickstarter PDF that is free for my readers to download.

Download it today to kickstart your journey!

https://www.subscribepage.com/iamsimplenaturallife kickstarter

I Am Simple Natural Life

"Don't reach for normal, reach for better."

— Michele Norris

INTRODUCTION

Welcome! I am so pleased you are here. This book is full of practical tips, thoughts, anecdotes, and suggestions of changes that you can make to enable you to live a more natural life. If you feel that your life is disconnected from nature, or you feel it is disjointed in any way, or perhaps you don't really know what exactly is wrong but something just doesn't feel quite right, then this book is for you.

Throughout the book, we will delve into all areas of your life from the very practical level, such as how to make natural products to clean your house, all the way through to integrating yoga and other holistic practices into your everyday life to improve your well-being and natural connection. There is something here for everyone, whatever stage of life you are at.

I have been on this journey of change for many years, most

rapidly for the past ten years. In my early life, I went through school and university, entered the business world within marketing, and climbed the corporate ladder. I had always been interested in more natural ways of living, but I was immersed in my business life and being successful within that world.

I only paused to take a breath when I had my first baby. Having a child changed my perceptions radically. And taking that break out of the workplace opened my eyes to a different way of living life—a more naturally balanced way of life. I began working from home as a freelance copywriter and started to find a more natural balance to my life. I now have four girls ages 10, 9, 8, and 7, and I write books from home. I am successful, but the way I define success is now very different. Financial success is still very important to me but so too is the balance of my life and my place within nature.

I have structured this book along the same pathway of the journey I have taken. I started on the path towards a more natural way of living with simple changes—less chemical-based household cleaners, reducing plastic waste, etc.—and I include lots of tips for this in Section One of the book. This first section is where you will find practical ideas for changes you can make within your household.

My journey then developed into bigger lifestyle changes. This was more of an organic change that occurred gradually, from the way I parent, to thinking about how to educate the children, through to living more seasonally. These changes took place slowly over time, and you will find all the details in Section Two. In this second section, I talk about the areas of my life that I have made changes within, the reasons why, and what to consider if you are drawn to make bigger lifestyle changes to achieve a more naturally balanced life.

And then I started looking after myself—my mind, body, and soul—as more of a priority. As any busy mum will know, self-care often comes last. And when I had four children under the age of three and a half, my self-care was pretty non-existent. But I have since taken steps to change this and now incorporate many aspects of well-being and self-care into my day. I eventually came to the realisation that in looking after myself, I can look after everyone else better. But it took me a while to understand this and even longer to implement it! So, in Section Three, we look at ways to care for yourself and to build self-care practices into your week so that your well-being improves and you can start to restore your natural connection. I will tell you about what has worked for me and how I have built up the different elements of self-care over time.

By way of background, let me tell you a little bit more about my family life, as I think it will help you understand things as you read through the book. I am married to Alex, who works as an IT testing contractor, and we live with our four girls in the UK. Our children are Enid (aged 10), Emily (aged 9), Alice (aged 8), and Florence (aged 7).

Enid has Cri du Chat syndrome (5P- syndrome), which means she is severely disabled both mentally and physically.

At age 10, she has limited walking ability and she cannot speak. She attends a special school where they help her to learn the skills she will need through life, but she will never be truly independent. She loves fashion, magazines, and music. Emily, Alice, and Florence are home educated. Emily, aged 9, attended school for just over a year before we decided to home educate her. She loves all things technology and makes amazing movies and clips utilising all manner of media. She is a real empath and has a sensitive soul. Alice, aged 8, has high-functioning autism (Asperger's), and we first investigated home education as an option due to the difficulties she would face within a traditional school environment. I talk more about home education in Section Two. Alice has so many interests and will devour every book she can lay her hands on about any of the topics she is interested in. Recently she has been most interested in learning about British birds and the solar system. Florence, aged 7, has never attended school. She is feisty and easy-going in equal measure. She has a keen sense of justice and is not afraid to speak her mind. She loves sports and being active, as well as spending time together reading stories.

So that's us! As a family we enjoy travelling, canoeing, nature documentaries, and getting outside into the countryside.

Throughout the book, you will notice three markers: "Imperfection Tips", "Imperfection Alerts" and "Imperfection Ideas". These stem from my fundamental message, which is not to worry about doing things perfectly. If you wait to make changes until you can implement everything perfectly, then you'll never do anything at all. It is far better to make some changes, however imperfectly, than to make none at all. "Imperfection Tips" will give you ideas and practical help for ways you can implement easy changes to your own life. "Imperfection Alerts" are where I tell you about my own experiences and the lessons I learned along the way. I hope these help you realise that (a) I am not perfect either, and (b) my real-life experiences may help give you an idea of how you could implement the changes within your own life. I finish each segment of the book with "Imperfection Ideas" which act as a checklist of quick and easy suggestions of things you could try in your life to get going with it right now.

My other key message throughout the book is to accept that your life is likely to be full of contradictions and not to worry about it! Perhaps you don't use any single-use plastic, but you fly to go on holiday twice a year. Perhaps you only eat seasonal food, but you spend very little time outside of the office connecting with nature. Perhaps you use only natural toiletries, but use disposable nappies for your baby. This book is not about aiming for perfection, but to make some level of change, however small and imperfectly, within your current life to improve your natural connection. It is not realistic to be able to do everything and to do it all perfectly. This book will help you identify the areas in your life that are most important to you and that are manageable to make changes, and to show you how to focus on them as a priority.

As a wise friend once told me, "Done is better than

perfect." It is not possible for most of us to create the completely perfect, natural life. But what we can all do, whatever our lifestyle and schedule, is to make simple, easy changes that improve what we are doing and move us closer to the natural life that we crave.

So, with that in mind, let's get started!

SECTION ONE: HOUSEHOLD

In this first section, we are going to look at some of the changes you can make within your household that can enable you to live more naturally. We are looking at physical, functional changes from the packaging your products come in, to what cleaning products you use, thinking about the toiletries you purchase, and looking at growing your own food. Remember, we are not aiming for perfection! Just read through and see what you are drawn to. Small changes are all you need to kickstart your journey towards a more naturally aligned life. Are you ready?

Grow Your Own

I dream one day of a Mr. McGregor style vegetable patch in what will be my huge garden with all the space (and time) in the world for self-sufficiency. Back to reality, I have just a small garden, and a big corner of that is filled with a trampoline, and another corner with a shed full of kids bikes and toys. But there is something about growing some of my own fruit and vegetables that really excites me. I feel wholesome and closer to nature. So, even in just the small space I have available (about 14 square metres, plus pots), this year I have grown the following food:

- Courgettes (zucchini)
- Cucumber
- Lettuce
- Tomatoes
- Butternut squash
- Sweet peppers (bell)
- Raspberries
- Purple sprouting broccoli
- Onions
- Apples
- Rhubarb
- Sugar-snap peas
- Beetroot (beets)
- Mini corn
- Fennel
- Strawberries
- Mint
- Coriander (cilantro)
- Parsley
- Thyme
- Rosemary
- Sage

- Basil
- Borage
- Nasturtiums
- Sunflowers
- Runner beans (string beans)
- Potatoes
- Spring onions (scallions)
- Salad leaves
- Baby spinach

Phew! I didn't actually realise quite how much I had grown until I listed it all there! Now, I didn't start off with all this. Remember it is all about the small steps. Around six years ago, I started growing a few bits and bobs in pots. With four tiny children at home (my eldest was three and a half when my youngest was born), and with the builders in doing an extension at the same time, the reality was that there was zero time for weeding and proper gardening. But, because it was important to me, I could just about find time to shove some soil in a few pots and grow a little bit. So I started with salad leaves, baby spinach, and radishes, all really quick and easy to grow, requiring no maintenance. Perfect!

Then, in time, we put in a mini apple tree and a rhubarb plant—they also just do their own thing and don't really need tending to.

Imperfection Alert: We have had the rhubarb plant for maybe five years now, and it was only this year I found out they like to be watered, regularly. I had never, ever, really really never, watered it. But even with that, it was still alive and still giving us a small batch of rhubarb to pick every year. I tell you this to show you how easy and low maintenance growing your own fruit and vegetables can be, and as a reminder that it is ok to get things wrong!

Gradually over the past few years I have grown a bit more and a bit more. I am still a minimal-time, haphazard kind of a gardener. I pay little attention to those instructions on the seed packets that tell you to give each plant a gazillion centimetres of space. Just do what feels right for you and that works in the space that you have.

So, to get started, think about two things:

1) In the space you have, what can you realistically fit in there? Remember it is possible to fit a lot in to a small space, as I have shown. I have squeezed more in by growing a lot of things vertically this year.
2) What do you like to eat? Not to state the obvious, but if you rarely eat salad there really isn't much point growing lots of lettuces for example.

Remember, we are not aiming for self-sufficiency here (though that would be nice one day). You are just looking to make a start. I began with only a couple of pots, and six years later I have the massive list of fruit and vegetables you saw before. Self-sufficiency is not a possibility with the space I have, but even with the small space I do have, so far this summer I haven't needed to buy any salad leaves, lettuces, strawberries, or sugar-snap peas. I cannot wait for my cucumbers and tomatoes to really get going in a few weeks!

Outside of these two key questions, when deciding what to grow, you could also consider the price of the fruit and vegetables you eat. Cherries is one that first comes to mind as an example—cherries can be super expensive in the shops, so why not plant a cherry tree (you can also get miniature varieties if space is tight) and save yourself some money? Our strawberry plants went crazy this summer and fed our family of six with all the strawberries we could eat for many weeks; it will have saved us a small fortune!

You could also make your choices about what to grow with a thought towards the packaging that your favourite products come in. For example, I really struggle to find sugar-snap peas without the little plastic trays and wrapped in film. So by growing them this year, I have saved not only money on what I would usually buy for our salads and stir frys, but I have also avoided the plastic packaging (more on that next). Happy days!

Imperfection Tip: Just grow something! Whether it's some basil on your windowsill or an entire walled kitchen garden. Grab some soil, get some seeds, and give it a go. For me it was a first step towards feeling more aligned with the natural world.

Imperfection Ideas:

Investigate what you can grow right now and grow at least one thing.

\# Look at what you can grow in the Spring, decide on three and set yourself a reminder in your phone.

\# Think about your ideal perfect life, what would you grow then? List everything you would grow. Then order the list in terms of your current practicalities (consider space and time). Aim to start growing things from the top of the list and gradually work your way down the list.

Packaging

This is a biggie and one where a lot of people start their journey. Small changes really can make a huge difference here.

Back when I was a child in the 80/90s, I can remember recycling was starting to be quite a big thing. One of my favourite things to do was taking a trip to the bottle bank and posting the bottles in through the little slots and hearing them smash as they landed in the container. So satisfying! And I have a vague recollection of using some kind of fridge magnet, which would show if a can was aluminium and if it could be recycled. It was all quite exciting (or maybe I was an odd child ...).

It also made us all feel better as the years rolled on and our products became more and more packaged; there was nothing to worry about as we could just pop the packaging into the recycling and it would be whisked away to a new life of infinite possibilities. Recycle your glass, paper, plastic and cans, and you can be sure you are doing your bit for the environment. Right?

Fast forward to the last couple of years where we have become increasingly aware that this recycling nirvana is not quite what we were led to believe. We have seen images of countries like Malaysia filled with our recycling that we have been shipping off for processing around the world. China has now closed their doors to taking our waste. The reality is that we produce far too much packaging and we don't have the facilities, not at home or elsewhere in the world, to process it all.

It isn't that recycling is a bad thing. But actually it isn't where our focus should be. Instead I have a new mantra for you to remember: Refuse. Reduce. Reuse. Recycle.

Refuse—Do you actually want and need the product?

Reduce—Is there a way to get the product without the packaging, or is there a way to reduce the amount of the product you buy?

Reuse—Once you have purchased the product and have the packaging, is there another way you can repurpose it?

Recycle—Only now when you have exhausted all the other options, should you think about recycling.

Let's take a practical example. Say that my children love hot chocolate and want me to buy some drinking chocolate powder. This is how my thought process could work. And remember, this is my own personal thought process about what I am happy with; this could look very different for each person. The point is not whether you agree with my choices but how you could reach your own decisions following the "Refuse, Reduce, Reuse, Recycle" mantra.

Option One—Refuse. Do we actually need this chocolate powder? Well, no, as humans we can live without hot chocolate. But. The kids really love it and it is important to them. It is better health-wise and also packaging-wise than an alternative of bottles of fizzy sodas that they might also like. One pot of powder makes multiple drinks, so that is a plus. So, on balance, I think this is a product that I am happy to purchase in this instance.

Option Two—Reduce. Are there any shops locally where we could buy this powder loose and fill our own containers? For me, in this case, there isn't. Is there anywhere online I can buy this powder in bulk? It would still come in packaging but there would less packaging if I bought a larger quantity in one container. For me, in this case, again there isn't. However, in the supermarket the powder comes in a small tub or a large tub, so I select the large tub to slightly reduce the waste packaging.

Option Three—Reuse. Hmm. A round 500g tub. Metal at the bottom, lined card around the sides. Could be used for a child's craft? Hello space rocket. Or you could get crafty yourself and turn it into a pen pot. Could it be used for future food storage options? In my case, I have used these empty containers as herb pots. I use a hammer and nail to knock a couple of holes in the metal bottom, fill with soil, pop in some seeds, and now I have a pretty cool looking herb garden in little matching chocolate powder pots.

Option Four—Recycle. If you have exhausted every other option then this is the point where you would recycle. And even if you have repurposed the container in option three, eventually when you have finished with the pot in whatever way you have used it, it can then be put in the recycling.

You are not going to get it right every time. Sometimes price can be an issue—unfortunately, loose products can often cost more (though I have noticed an improvement on this recently for many loose fruit and veg from the supermarket). Sometimes time is an issue—you just need X product right now and don't have the necessary headspace to think the purchase through fully. You may be in the supermarket being pestered by the kids "Can we have this? Can we have this? Can we have this?" Repeat infinitum ...

But ultimately, the aim is to keep the "Refuse, Reduce, Reuse, Recycle" mantra in mind and move towards making more conscious, mindful choices wherever you can.

And as ever, it is ok to start small. Think of one product that you buy a lot of and go through the mantra. Could you find a suitable alternative way to buy the product? Is there a way you could repurpose the packaging? Or perhaps a product you use has packaging that cannot even be recycled, can you source an alternative that has more environmentally-friendly credentials?

Imperfection Tip: Stop buying water in plastic bottles; in the UK the average person uses around 150 plastic bottles every year, in the U.S. that figure rises to around 167 bottles. Get yourself a reusable water bottle that you can refill instead. This is a really quick and easy change to make.

And if you regularly buy take out coffee, get yourself a reusable coffee cup. Many cafes even offer a small discount for using your own cup.

Imperfection Alert: Here is a real example from my own life where I gradually made a change. Every week we were buying big multipacks of crisps (chips). This was a problem to me on two levels—firstly, crisps aren't the healthiest of snacks and we had fallen into a routine of each having a bag every day. Secondly, all those bags every week of hard-to-recycle materials really bothered me. Gah!

Now, I could have just stopped buying the crisps. Job done. Except, that doesn't sit right with me. It wasn't just me eating the crisps, everyone in the family was enjoying them, and as you'll learn in later sections, it is important to me that everyone in the family has a say over what impacts their lives. So, I wasn't comfortable with just removing the crisps from everyone. I considered "eco-bricking" them, but the thought of washing out all the packs, getting them perfectly dry, cutting them in to tiny pieces, and then ramming them in to plastic bottles with the end of a wooden spoon just didn't appeal, and I couldn't think of what I would do eventually with all my packed-up bottles either. Eco-bricking wasn't the option for me. So instead, I started buying the big share bags of crisps. People could take a bowlful when they wanted and it meant that while we were still creating hard-to-recycle waste, we were creating less of it.

And what happened was that because we had broken the routine of taking a bag of crisps every day, getting a bowlful was enough of a difference to our habit to actually break that daily routine we each had. Gradually we were eating less crisps. And soon we would just have a bag between us with lunch on a Saturday, and then we started having something different on a Saturday that crisps didn't really go with, and suddenly ... we aren't buying crisps regularly anymore and none of us have missed them.

I hope my example here helps show you that it's ok to move slow and imperfectly. In the end, you will move to where you want to get to and it doesn't have to be an uncomfortable journey. Do what feels right for you and your situation.

Imperfection Tip: Be mindful of freebies. We all love something that is free, but before you take it just "because it was free," stop and think—do you actually want or need what they are giving away? Make it a conscious choice.

If buying loose products is too expensive for you, consider buying in bulk to reduce the packaging you buy without increasing the overall cost.

Imperfection Ideas:

\# Look around your kitchen. How much unrecyclable waste is there? Choose one item to switch out to an alternative.

\# Buy a refillable water bottle.

\# Commit to reusing as many items of your current packaging as you can. Get creative!

\# Investigate where your nearest refill shop is. Is there somewhere you can visit where you are able to refill your own containers for some of your produce?

\# Decide on one fruit or vegetable that you will only buy loose.

Food Storage

Another area to consider and that is easy to get started with is food storage. Think about how you store leftover food—are you wrapping it in cling film (plastic/saran wrap)? Instead of this plastic, one-use film, there is a range of different things you can use. Wax wraps are fabric coated in bees wax (or a vegan alternative) and it then works the same plastic wrap. You simply cover the dish or the food and it holds itself in place. You can then wipe or wash the wrap down afterwards for reuse.

Or, keeping it really simple, you can go back to basics with a plate placed over a bowl to keep things fresh in the fridge. I use a lot of air-tight plastic boxes at home; you can also use metal boxes, which look nice and last well.

Imperfection Tip: Wax wraps can be expensive but you can easily make your own. Take a piece of fabric and lay it on an old baking tray, grate wax onto the surface of the fabric and then put into a medium to high oven to melt the wax. Keep an eye on it in the oven and when all the wax has melted, take it out straightaway otherwise it could burn. Peel the fabric off the baking tray and gently wave it for a couple of seconds until it is dried. Note: It is best to use an old baking tray as they can be hard to clean afterwards.

Wax wraps make really special gifts too! If you want to make it look extra nice, cut the edges of your fabric with pinking shears before you apply the wax. This will prevent any frayed edges.

You can use wax wraps not only for food storage in the home but also to wrap sandwiches and similar foods you want to take out with you. However, what I use for sandwiches just because I find them so handy are specific sandwich wraps. These are essentially a square of fabric sewn together with a square of waterproof material and then a piece of Velcro to secure it in place when it's wrapped around the sandwich. These are just fab. They open out with the sandwich inside to then provide a little picnic placemat where you can put on some crisps or other picnic bits, and it keeps the grass and leaves off your food. They make picnics a lot more manageable with multiple children! I can then wipe the wraps down or pop them on to a cold-water wash in the washing machine and, voila, we have them ready to use for another day.

No more foil, no more plastic wrap. Wax wraps and sandwich wrappers are a sure win!

Imperfection Alert: I sometimes buy frozen fruit from the supermarket. You know the resealable bags with frozen raspberries, strawberries, or blueberries, etc.? I don't like the fact that they come in these plastic bags. However, I don't have the garden space to grow all the fruit we eat, and the frozen fruit works well to make a fruit compote for a healthier yoghurt. So, excuses out of the way, what I do is wash out the bags when I have finished the fruit and I then have a little stash of reusable, resealable bags I can use for other purposes. They are great for storing left over soup in the freezer. I use them for taking grapes or other loose fruit with us on picnics. I actually also use them when we go away as a wash bag for our toothbrushes. Versatile eh?! So, while in an ideal world I would prefer not to have the bags in the first place, I do reuse them many more times in various guises.

Imperfection Tip: What products do you buy that you don't have an easy alternative for? Is there a way you can find to reutilise the packaging the products come in?

Imperfection Ideas:

Switch out to one reusable – could be wax wraps, or a sandwich wrapper perhaps.

Look at the existing packaging you buy. Could you reuse any of this as further food storage?

Try not using foil or plastic wrap for one week – see what creative alternatives you can come up with! Could you extend your first week to two weeks…? to a month…?

Cleaning

The world of household cleaners that we know is a mind-blowing array of chemicals and packaging. A spray for this, a spray for that, another spray for something else, a cream for this, a gel for that, and maybe even a powder. Plastic bottles and nozzles, and inside, well, goodness knows what. Looking at the information on the pack just leaves one more confused unless you happen to have a PhD in chemistry. The only certainty is that from all the warning labels on the packaging, you can be sure that whatever the product is inside the bottle, it isn't very natural! I even saw on a bottle the other day a warning that the product will cause active harm to sea life. It is completely baffling to me why manufacturers are even allowed to sell things like that, so you need to be mindful about what you are buying. Just because it is on the shelf doesn't mean it isn't harmful to the environment or your health.

The good news is, however, that you don't need all this stuff. You can be more environmentally friendly AND still have a clean home. The even better news is, you are likely to save yourself some money in the process too.

I started with laundry detergent. I was using a standard supermarket brand of detergent, and as I became more aware of the harm some of the chemicals contained within these standard products, I moved towards an "environmentally friendly" marketed brand. It cost more money, and now in hindsight I am not sure how environmentally friendly many of these green-branded products really are, but it was a step in the right direction.

I continued merrily like this for a number of years, and then I discovered soap nuts. Soap nuts grow on the soap berry tree in the Himalayas and contain something called saponin, which is a natural surfactant (shop-bought detergents contain chemical surfactants). Simply pop a few soap nuts in a bag with your washing, put the machine on, and voila, you have clean clothes. Really. Really. Really. Five soap nuts in a bag will last at least 10 washes, I use mine for more. I buy the soap nuts in a big bag and it lasts me for years. You don't need any softener either. The soap nuts have a naturally softening effect.

Imperfection Tip: Despite the name, soap nuts are not nuts at all. So they are suitable for nut allergy sufferers. Soap nuts are really a berry, and you might sometimes see them called soap berries.

If you would rather source something closer to home, apparently good old horse chestnuts (conkers) also have similar cleaning properties.

Imperfection Alert: I haven't yet tried using horse chestnuts myself as we are bizarrely short on horse chestnut trees where I live, but one day perhaps I'll find the time to trek out to collect enough and give it a go. I think in the case of conkers you need to boil them first to make a liquid, so this extra step is also a deterrent for me and my lazy approach to life, however, it isn't insurmountable, and I'm sure when the time is right I'll give it a go.

If you can't quite bring yourself at this stage to get rid of your powdered or liquid laundry detergent, a really easy change is to remove your usual fabric softener and replace it with white vinegar. It is super cheap and easy to get hold of and will do the same job as your softener, just without all the chemicals. And don't worry, your clothes won't smell of vinegar!

Imperfection Tip: You can get white vinegar in most supermarkets in one-pint glass bottles. Or to save even more money, look at buying a large container and decanting what you need into a smaller bottle.

In the bathroom and kitchen, instead of having various

cleaning sprays, all you need is to dilute white vinegar and water, and pop it into an empty spray bottle. And there you have an effective multi-purpose cleaner. The smell can be a bit vinegary, so if this bothers you, just pop in a citrus peel of your choice.

For any stains that need a bit of extra oomph, sprinkle bicarbonate of soda (baking soda) on them first. Goodbye cream cleaner!

Perhaps even these simple changes are just a bit too much hard work for you? If that's the case, here is my ultimate lazy trade. Are you ready for it? Drum roll please ... Reusable cloths. That's right folks. Reusable cloths. Simple, simple, simple. Instead of using kitchen towels or disposable cloths, buy (or even make if you are nifty with the sewing machine) cloths that can be washed and reused. This one simple swap will stop you sending heaps of waste to landfill and will save you money at the same time.

Don't bother with chemical sprays for dusting; a damp cloth will do the job. Then wash it and use it again when you need. I do the same for dish cloths. Previously I would buy disposable dish cloths, but now I just have a pile of cloths and use one of those for the dishes or to wipe up spills. Then when you have enough dirty ones, just pop them in the wash with your other towels and tea towels.

Imperfection Tip: Speaking of reusable cloths, I used reusable wet wipes for my children—and am still using the same set ten years later. Worldwide we use around 450 billion disposable wet wipes every year. At best they end up in landfill; flushed disposable wipes end up blocking pipes and sewage systems.

And yet, reusable wipes are so easy. I keep them wet in a box in the bathroom. Used ones go in a net bag in a bin, which, when full, I wash in the washing machine. Easy peasy. If you have kids and want to make an easy change, this one could be a game changer for you. Also, the same for make-up remover pads. And the same too for sanitary towels and period pants. Seriously, if you haven't yet entered the world of reusables, take a step in today. It will be revolutionary for your life.

Imperfection Ideas:

\# Choose one household cleaner or detergent and swap it out to an eco-brand or natural alternative.

\# Keep your next spray bottle when the cleaner runs out with a view to using it to try a natural homemade alternative.

\# Buy or make some cloths that you can re-use. Which would make the biggest difference in your household – e.g. disposable wipes, kitchen towels or cleaning cloths? Start there.

Menstrual Products

Did you know there are four carrier bags worth of plastic in every single disposable sanitary towel? And even tampons contain plastic too; around six percent of a tampon is plastic. With this in mind, think how much plastic is being thrown away every month. Here is a yuck fact—there is actually more plastic sanitary waste washed up on Europe's beaches every year than plastic straws or single use coffee cups. That's pretty disgusting, not to mention harmful.

So if you stopped using these products, think what an immediate impact that would have to reducing your plastic waste. This is a really easy change to make in your life as there are lots of alternative products available. In the world of reusable sanitary items, we can group products into three sections—reusable sanitary towels, menstrual cups, and period pants. And the good news is that over my lifetime, I have used them all so I can help you out a bit here with the pros and cons. Everyone's body is different though, so you'll need to see what works best for you.

Menstrual cups—These are little silicone, rubber, or flexible plastic cups that sit inside your vagina and collect the blood inside you. So they work in a similar way as tampons. The cup collects the blood and then you empty it out into the toilet (or some people actually keep the blood to pour on their plants!), rinse it out with water, and reinsert. At the end of your bleeding, you simply clean it (I use a gentle washing up liquid) and sterilise it (I just boil it in water for five to seven minutes). And then when it's dry, put it away until your next period.

Sanitary towels—These work the same as the disposable sanitary towels you buy in the supermarket, but they usually have a popper to attach around your underwear instead of a sticky pad. You then wash them in the washing machine, dry, and use again. And again. And again. Because I already use rewashable wipes as mentioned before, I just put my used sanitary towels in with the wipes and wash them together. You can buy special little bags to store used towels in though if that works better for you.

Period pants—Oh lovely, lovely period pants. I am new to period pants, but I have to admit they are my new best friend. With period pants, they work similarly to a sanitary towel but the absorbent pad is within the underwear. Depending on the pants, they can hold up to four tampons worth of blood, and you can wear them for around eight hours or so before they need to be changed, and then you just wash them on a 40 degree wash and leave to dry naturally.

Pros and cons of each in my experience:

Menstrual Cups

- They are a great replacement if you like tampons.
- They are good if you want to go swimming and you bleed heavily.
- They can be a bit fiddly to get in the right position until you get practiced with them. You might need to persevere.

- You may get a small amount of leakage during certain times of your bleed (for me it seems to depend on what position my cervix is in).
- You do need to be willing to put your fingers up inside you to position the cup.

Sanitary Towels

- They are good for you if you don't like internal sanitary products.
- They are good for the times during your bleed where your cervix moves lower and the cup may feel uncomfortable.
- They are good as extra protection alongside a cup if you find you leak at all with a cup.
- I find they can slide up your underwear a bit, which is annoying, but that could be the brands I have tried.

Period Pants

- They don't move around and are very comfortable.
- They can collect all the blood from your cycle, or you can also use them as a backup to cup leakages (I am a heavy bleeder, and I use them as a standalone product without any problem).
- They are the most expensive option here. However, you will still save money in the long run rather than buying disposable products every month.
- You can also get period swimwear too.
- Did I mention period pants are my new best friend?

Imperfection Tip: This is such an easy area of your life to make a change. There are products available to suit everyone, and with every month you don't buy disposable products, you are saving a whole heap of wasteful plastic, and you are saving yourself money in the long run too. Win-win!

Imperfection Ideas:

Think about your lifestyle and the menstrual products you currently use. What would be the best type of product for you or would a mixture make sense?

Investigate one type of reusable to start with, consider how it could work for you in your usual day to day.

Look at different suppliers of your chosen reusable – decide which you would choose.

Bite the bullet! Buy the reusable and try it. Commit to trialling it for three months. (And remember you don't have to ditch your current products immediately, you could start by trying the reusables when you are at home and stick with your current product when you are out and about if you are unsure and it gives you more confidence to start with).

Cosmetics and Toiletries

Most of the products we use on our faces and bodies are unnecessary. There, I've said it. We spend a huge amount of money every year on products that are not needed, and many are full of stuff that is seeping into our skin that we don't even fully know what its effects are. Added to this is the reality that many of these products come in unrecyclable packaging, so I think you can guess that overall I am not a huge fan.

- **Cosmetics**

At this point, I will be honest and tell you, I don't even wear makeup. I used to. I am a woman, and I am naturally a very compliant person. As a woman, you are supposed to wear makeup, or at least that's what the adverts tell us. So, of course, I did. For a while I even kind of enjoyed it—I think more the ritual of sitting quietly and doing something for myself. I did not enjoy the taking it off at the end of the day. Or the taking it off in the morning because I forgot the night before (OK, so I didn't forget, I just couldn't be bothered; I told you I am lazy!).

But as time went on, it really started to grate on me that there was this expectation placed on me as a woman that I *should* wear makeup. Just because I am a woman and not a man. So I missed days here and there, and got generally a bit lazy with my make-up routine. And then I had children. Four girls born within three and a half years of each other. As a mum, I was rarely going out, and as I was now working from home, I didn't need to put makeup on to go to the office or places like it. So the girls rarely saw me in makeup.

And then one day I was going to a fancy evening event for charity, and I started putting makeup on, and my then four-year-old was watching me fascinated as it was probably the first time she had properly witnessed me doing this. She was quizzing me on what I was doing and why. And that's when the penny dropped. Why WAS I doing this? If I am telling her she doesn't need it, but I am putting it on my own face, what am I saying about how I feel about me? And from that point on, I haven't worn any makeup.

I am not suggesting that this is something you yourself should necessarily do, but there is no harm in considering the reasons behind the choices you are making. Are you putting the makeup on habitually without thought? Perhaps take the time to think about whether your habits still serve you. And if they do, when you are considering what to purchase, think about the mantra we looked at earlier— Refuse, Reduce, Reuse, Recycle. It doesn't have to be all or nothing, every person's journey is different, but just think about what you are doing, why you are doing it, and if there are any easy changes you can make. Remember, small steps are good enough.

Imperfection Tip: If you habitually wear makeup every day, then why not consider only wearing makeup for work and giving your skin a break on the weekends? Or try going makeup free on your next holiday.

- **Toiletries**

With the toiletries I use, I have one rule: If I wouldn't put it IN my body then I don't use it ON my body. Around 60 percent of what we put on our skin is absorbed into our bodies. So it is really important that you know what you are using.

My number one toiletry item is coconut oil. I like coconut oil for a few reasons:

1) I would eat it, so it ticks that priority box for me.

2) It is versatile—I use it as a face, body, and hand moisturiser, and also a lip balm. If I wore makeup, then it also works as an effective makeup remover.

3) It is easy to buy in glass jars rather than plastic containers, and I can reuse the glass jars for other things.

4) It is inexpensive. Well, you can find coconut oil to suit any budget, handily for me I don't really like the scent of coconut so I actually use the no-odour varieties, which tend to be cheaper.

Imperfection Tip: Try coconut oil instead of your usual moisturisers, lip balm, and makeup remover—just give it a go. Maybe try it when you next go away on holiday. Just think how much lighter your luggage could be without all your usual products!

- **Deodorants and Antiperspirants**

There is a two-fold reason for considering ditching your deodorants and antiperspirants. The first is simply because of the packaging they come in, which is usually not recyclable and ends up in landfill, but there is also a health reason as well. Did you know that your usual antiperspirant could be increasing your risk of breast cancer? There is a link between antiperspirants that contain aluminium and breast cancer. The risk seems to be greatest for those who shave their armpits and then apply the antiperspirant. Over the last fifty years or so, there has been an increased proportion of breast cancers being found in the upper corner of the breast (close to the armpit). And what research shows is that while a minimal amount of aluminium is typically absorbed through the skin, when you shave, not only do you remove the hairs but you are also removing a thin layer of skin and this means aluminium is then being absorbed in through this area. So you could stop shaving, or you could stop using these products containing aluminium, which is toxic to your body.

There are many natural alternative products available, which usually come in a cardboard tube or a glass jar, depending on their format. And these products, while better for the environment, also do not come with the potential health risks of your aluminium-containing products.

Imperfection Tip: Worried that you might smell if you stop using antiperspirant? Ironically, antiperspirants actually increase the types of bacteria that cause us to smell. The more we use, the more we need them. It is a vicious cycle. Do, however, be aware that your body will need to adjust when you stop using antiperspirants. I used natural deodorant alternatives for quite a while, then moved to a salt stick, and in the last year haven't used any product at all. And I don't smell.

If you are not sure if your current product contains aluminium, look out for the ingredients aluminium chloralhydrate or aluminium zirconium tetrachlorohydrex gly. These are what you need to avoid.

Imperfection Alert: I am a sweaty person. I used to use the strongest anti-perspirant on the market. If I didn't I would have sweat patches, I would think I smelled—I am not sure if I did or not, but I didn't feel pleasant. And so for years and years I just carried on with the antiperspirant, because, well, what option did I have? And then one day I didn't. And I just tried a natural product. I didn't feel it worked to stop me sweating, but that's because it doesn't! It isn't meant to. Your body sweats for a reason, preventing it doing so is not a good thing. And once I got that in my head and understood the process a bit more, the transition to natural deodorant, and then to using nothing, was a lot easier.

By switching to a natural deodorant, you will be making a better choice for the environment and a better choice for your health. It's a no-brainer.

Imperfection Tip: And while we are on the subject of our armpits ... swap out your disposable razor for a safety razor. With a safety razor, you just replace the actual metal blade rather than the entire casing, or even the entire razor, as is the case with many disposable options. It works just as well (better actually in my opinion), and the blades are easy to change. Minimal waste plus minimal fuss equals an easy change to make.

- **Hair Care**

I haven't used shampoo for years. Really. I haven't. This one was a long on-and-off journey for me. Are you sitting comfortably? Then I will begin ...

I realised in my early twenties that most shampoos were full of chemical yuckiness (that's my technical term). So for many years I bought more natural shampoos and then moved to shampoo bars. That was great. Then I had children and I slipped back to the quicker choice of supermarket-bought shampoos, and I had some dandruff so I needed special shampoo to deal with that. I only washed the children's hair in water, because I knew that's all babies' hair needs. But somehow I didn't make the link to my own head. And then one day it just fell back on to my radar again, and it was like a lightbulb moment.

I researched and researched—some might call it procrastination—and then one day that was it. I went for it. I just stopped using shampoo. For the kids and my husband, they use water, followed by a natural conditioner. For me, I need something with a bit more kick to it than just water so I use bicarbonate of soda mixed with water, or sometimes a soap nut solution, or occasionally gram flour and water made into a paste. And then instead of conditioner, I use diluted apple cider vinegar. My hair is nice and clean, and since going "no-poo," I don't have dandruff anymore either. I guess my scalp was reacting to something in either the shampoo or conditioner I was using.

Imperfection Tip: There are many different options of ingredients you can use instead of shampoo and conditioner. It is a case of trial and error to find the best ingredients that work for your hair.

The transition away from shampoo can be a bit scary. I won't lie, you need to expect a few weeks (and actually, I was unlucky, for me it was a few months) of slightly yuck hair. Nothing a ponytail couldn't hide though. It helps to understand the science behind what is going on. Your body produces sebum, a natural oil that keeps your hair clean. When you use shampoo, you wash all the sebum away and your body thinks, "Oh heck, we are out of sebum!" So it makes even more to compensate, which makes your hair feel greasy, so you wash it with shampoo again, and hey presto you are locked into your very own over-producing sebum vicious circle.

When you give up shampoo, you have to go through a certain amount of time with your body over-producing sebum before it realises, "Hey, no one is taking all this sebum away, we can slow up on the production now guys."

So that will be your slight yuck period. But then, if you can persevere, oh my, you will be rewarded with naturally clean, glossy hair forever more! And you'll also notice that the frequency that you need to wash your hair becomes less and less. I don't *need* to wash my hair now for around 10 days. I know! We recently travelled for three months and I can't tell you how grateful I was not to have to be worried about washing my hair every day, especially as we were often in areas with low water reserves.

I know this won't be for everyone, and if it isn't for you right now then that's ok. But why not look into a more natural shampoo, or try a shampoo bar? Small steps towards a bigger end goal.

Imperfection Tip: Use solid shampoo bars instead of liquid shampoo. Think how many plastic bottles you could reduce by each year. You could also try soap bars rather than liquid soap dispensers for washing your hands. Small changes can add up to a big difference.

And another thing to consider, if going shampoo-free is too scary right now, what about the other products you use on your hair? There are often natural alternatives—flax seeds make an easy hair gel substitute, bees wax and coconut oil make a great hair wax, you can even use citrus to make a natural but effective hair spray.

Imperfection Tip: To make the flax-seed gel, take a quarter cup of flax seeds (also called linseeds) and put in a pan with one cup of water. Bring to the boil, stirring occasionally, and then leave to simmer for five minutes. Strain the liquid into a container and there you have your gel. Play around with the timings—the longer you simmer it for, the stronger the gel will be. The gel will store in the fridge for a good few days, you can also freeze it if you want to make a big batch and split it into use-sizes.

Hair dye is another scary area both in terms of the number of harsh chemicals we are placing on (and absorbing into) our bodies, and also rinsing out into the water supply. And yet equally scary is for many people to consider not using it! I used to dye my hair on and off, though I have never been a regular dyer. I started getting the odd grey hair during my twenties, and then increasingly so in my thirties. And this gradual greying gave me a lot of time to consider what I was going to do when the greys got "unmanageable". In the end, I came to a decision—and at the time it felt like a massive decision—to go grey naturally.

For now, I have an Anna-from-Frozen-like strip of grey running down the front section, and you know what? I love it! I think of it as my wisdom, and it will grow bigger and spread as I grow older. However, it took me many years of soul searching to come to that place of acceptance. And I understand how hard it is to go against the grain of society's expectation, especially as a woman, to hide the aging process. Women are expected to look a certain way, and that way is not grey. So if you are not ready to go au natural then what can you do?

First of all, make sure you know what is going onto your hair and remember that on your hair also means in your body. Many of the chemicals used in hair dye can cause skin reactions—that's why you are supposed to do a patch test first to check your reaction and also wear gloves to limit the skin toxicity of the hair dye. But even if your body isn't obviously reacting against the dye, it doesn't mean that the chemicals won't be doing damage.

As an alternative to chemical dyes, there are lots of natural hair dye products on the market. Henna is the obvious one that comes to mind as a natural hair dye, but you can also buy more sophisticated products that will dye your hair without the usual toxins. And if you really can't bear the thought of risking your colour by moving away from the chemicals, then at least find out what is in the dye you are using, and if possible, avoid p-Phenylenediamine (PPD), ammonia, phthalates, hydrogen peroxide, resorcinol, parabens, and lead acetate. If you are going to dye your hair, you really need to become ingredient-conscious and consider not only what could be going into your body but also what chemicals you are flushing into the water supply.

- **Oral Care**

I once heard something that literally stopped me in my tracks. My first-ever toothbrush that I had all those years ago when I was tiny, is still in existence somewhere in landfill. That thought just completely hit me in the stomach. And further than that, every single toothbrush that I have ever used is still in landfill. Think how many toothbrushes one person uses in a lifetime (I have seen estimates of around 300 toothbrushes on average), all sitting in landfill. That just floors me every time I think about it.

We use products, like toothbrushes, without a thought. We use them, we throw them away, and I didn't think anything of it. But that is an insane amount of plastic being thrown away with nowhere for it to go. The handle of most plastic toothbrushes is made from polypropylene and the bristles are usually nylon, another type of plastic. Both are sourced from non-renewable fossil fuels and do not biodegrade.

Bamboo toothbrushes make a really easy, great alternative. Bamboo is a fast growing, natural wood, and it is fully biodegradable. Bamboo toothbrushes are shaped the same as plastic toothbrushes, the only difference is the material they are made of, which means that your bamboo toothbrush can be composted and will decompose once you have disposed of it.

Imperfection Tip: Be careful to double check what the bristles are made of and how to dispose of them. Most bamboo toothbrushes still come with nylon (plastic) bristles—so they are not completely plastic free, though significantly less plastic is used than a traditional plastic toothbrush. You can get some bamboo toothbrushes that use boar hair instead, so completely plastic free, but not cruelty free. I am hopeful that if the demand for bamboo toothbrushes continues in the way we have seen over the last couple of years, that plastic free, cruelty free alternatives will soon be developed.

And what about toothpaste? Most shop-bought toothpastes come in plastic tubes—either those flexible tubes we squeeze or those solid upright containers with a pump. There are a wide range of plastic free alternatives to traditional toothpaste, available with or without fluoride. Glass jars of toothpaste are easy to find in minimal waste stores or on the Internet. And you can also buy toothpaste tablets and other format alternatives to traditional paste. Try them out and see what works for you.

Imperfection Alert: The first time I tried my natural toothpaste I was almost sick. Literally. It was vile! It was gritty, it looked a bit like mud, it tasted odd, and it just felt all wrong. It was completely disgusting. So, slightly traumatised, I put it to the back of the cupboard and ignored it for a couple of months. And then one day I felt the urge to try it again, and I did, and it was fine! I have no idea what the problem was for me the first time or what had changed for me by the second time. All I know is the toothpaste was nice to use and I still use the same brand to this day. Weird!

Imperfection Tip: If you are not yet feeling ready for natural toothpaste, then consider the packaging your current toothpaste comes in. Toothpaste tubes, through being flexible, somehow feel like they would be the better choice environmentally, but they are actually very difficult to recycle owing to a thin strip of metal on the inside of the packaging, which helps keep the toothpaste fresh. The solid containers are overall easier and more widely recycled.

Imperfection Ideas:

\# Commit to one day a week make-up free.

\# Find out what ingredients are in your hair dye.

\# Swap to an aluminium-free deodorant.

\# Make a swap to one natural alternative product – maybe try a bamboo toothbrush, a shampoo bar, or look at natural toothpastes.

- - Summary - -

I hope you can see just how easy it is to start making changes. Remember, we are not aiming for perfection, and we are not aiming to change everything all at the same time. What small step could you commit to? Will you swap out your menstrual products, stop using plastic wrap, start using natural household cleaners, or will you bite the bullet and go shampoo-free? The important thing is to make a start. By making a commitment to make just one change alters your brain patterns and opens your eyes to a whole new path and way of being. Just imagine where that first small step will take you.

SECTION TWO: LIFESTYLE

In this section, we start to look more deeply at how we actually live our lives. We are still working on a practical level, but looking at changes you could make within your day-to-day life that could bring more alignment and help you live more naturally. The same as with Section One, we are not aiming to change everything, and we are not aiming to make lots of big changes all in one go. But as you read through the sections, you may find that some ideas particularly interest you or resonate with you—focus on these. Come back to revisit the others at a later date.

Working and Living as One

For so many people, they live as though they have two lives. The life where they go off to work and do their "work stuff," and then the life at home where they do their "home stuff." This dual-life is compounded by the fact that so many of us work outside the home. But is this good for us to split our time and mind in this way? For most of us, home is where the heart is, it is where we feel most comfortable and at peace. What if you could bring those feelings of contentment into your work? What benefit would it have to your work output? And how would it improve your overall life and mental health?

When people talk about trying to achieve a good work/life balance, it makes me feel a bit uncomfortable. As an ambition it just misses the mark entirely. Why seek a balance? What about having one life, of which you enjoy all elements? There is no need to be negotiating between one side and the other and trying to balance them out. You could do what you enjoy in all areas of your life. Perhaps you currently spend your days working, looking forward to when you can get back to the things you love. If that's the case, then this section is definitely for you! But even if you enjoy your work, there could be benefit from blurring the edges of these two separate areas of your life.

Imperfection Alert: I started working from home around 11 years ago. I'll be honest, it wasn't so much a choice as a shove in that direction. I was made redundant when I was pregnant with my first baby, and the reality was that I was going to find it hard (almost impossible) to find a new job while pregnant. So I set up on my own, and I have never looked back! My finding-a-new-job options were also further limited when my first child was born with profound disabilities—child care options are limited (pretty non-existent) for families in these situations. But the redundancy that felt so unfair and poorly timed actually turned out to be the biggest gift I could have received. It gave me the opportunity to build work into my life that fit in with my new role as a mother at home. Without that redundancy, I would not be in the position I am today. I would not have been able to have the children so close in age as we wanted. I would not have been able to home educate the children. And I would not be living my dream as an author today. But enough about me. What about you?

What would changing your work or your working practices mean for you? Do you love your job? What is your calling? Taking all practicalities out of it, what do you dream of doing? If you don't take time to consider this, then you cannot know where you want to head towards, and your current reality will continue day to day. I recently heard someone talking that had given up a very successful career as a lawyer to become a fitness trainer. She said she realised that she was spending every day in the office looking forward to the 40 minutes at the end of the day when she could go for a run. Do you too live your day wishing you could be doing something different?

Imperfection Tip: Take ten minutes, a piece of paper and a pen, and just write whatever comes into your head. What do you enjoy doing? What lights you up? What does your dream life look like? Don't hold back or worry about what is practical. And if nothing comes to mind then that is ok too, just sit with that. Give yourself time. If you have had a lifetime of never daring to imagine how things could be different, it may not come to you straightaway. For others of you, you may instantly know what your dream life looks like. Wherever you are on your journey is just the place where you should be. Don't fight it. Work with it and get any ideas you have out on paper.

And when you have that, think—what changes could you make today? It doesn't have to be a grand gesture like going to your boss and resigning on the spot, but what small steps could you start to take towards your goal? Could you request more flexible working hours? Could you work partially from home? Could you sign yourself up for an evening course to retrain or to take you to the next stage you want to get to? Something as small as making the time to take a walk outside every lunch time rather than staying at your desk makes a big difference. Whatever steps you can take, however small, will bring happiness and more alignment in your life. Make a commitment to yourself to do what you can.

Whatever it looks like for you, just show up and do something. So many people walk through life as though blindfolded going to the same old job, doing the same old routine, knowing it doesn't fulfil them but never thinking they could have more. And I am here to tell you that everyone can have more. You just need to decide what that looks like for you, and start taking small steps towards it.

Any way that you can bring the feelings of warmth and contentment that you may feel in your home life into your work life will bring huge benefits to you and your happiness. When you consider how many hours you currently work outside of the house, doing something that potentially doesn't fill your cup, just imagine how good you would feel if you changed that up. No one will make this happen apart from you. Give yourself permission to dream big. You need to dream it to achieve it.

Imperfection Alert: We'll come back to my own example. By working for myself, I have been able to be at home to raise my four children (something that became very important to me as soon as I had my first child). I can arrange my own hours around our needs as a family. I can choose to work on the things that interest me. I guess you could say I have been lucky, and I do feel so lucky, but also it didn't just "happen." I made this my reality.

What could your new reality look like for you?

Imperfection Ideas:

\# Spend time thinking about your dream life. Write down whatever comes to mind – don't question it or censor it. Dream big!

\# What one small step could you take today that would start you on the journey towards your dream life?

\# What one BIG step could you work towards over the next few months? Plan out the steps you need to take each week. You need a plan!

Home Education—Specifically Unschooling

This for me is much the same as the work/home-life split. Schooling is such a normal part of our society that we rarely, if ever, stop to consider it as a concept. Children learn how to walk, how to talk, how to develop, up until the age of formal education. Here in the UK that is age four. And then suddenly at age four we decide that they need to be placed somewhere outside of the home and specifically taught skills and information. Their independent learning has got them so far, but somehow now they are four years old, they need to be taught. And so we put them into school and use systems of rewards and punishments to get them to do the learning that they need to do in order to be functional adults.

But what if that wasn't necessary? What if the independent learning that they did in early childhood could continue throughout their lives? Did you know that compulsory schooling has only been around for about 150 years? It is a relatively new concept, for the vast majority of our history as humans we have developed without the use of schools.

Surely though we need to teach children to read and write at the very least, otherwise we'll end up with illiterate young adults emerging from childhood? Well, actually, no, children will teach themselves to read. And to write. If they are raised in an environment with books available, if they are read to, in their own time they will read.

There is no specific "right time" for a child to do anything. Yet when our children enter school they enter a system, similar to a conveyor-belt factory system, where children of age five must learn X, and children of age nine must learn Y. But these children will naturally develop at different paces. And the fact is, not even different governments can agree when children "should" know different things. As I mentioned, in UK schools, children start formal education at age four and are taught to read from that age. In many other western countries, formal schooling doesn't start until age seven, and reading isn't taught until this age. So who is right? What is the perfect age to learn different skills? Could it be that there isn't actually a "perfect age" and it is dependent on the individual child?

Over the past twenty years, probably more, schooling has become increasingly measured and standardised. Schools need to show that they are teaching children what the government requires them to teach, so children are tested more and more. And actually, to enable the testing and means of measurement, what is taught is increasingly based upon what can be tested. There is an ever-increasing focus on maths, English, and science, with diminished time on the "arts" and sports; the curriculum becomes narrower in order for schools to be measured. It isn't actually about what we think children should know at all.

And the uncomfortable reality is that being taught something doesn't mean a child has learned it, hence the "summer slide" we know all too well where children forget much of what they were taught during the academic year. That is because they hadn't properly learned it in the first place. They were taught it, they were tested on it—they maybe even have passed the test really well—but then they forgot it. I am sure we all have experience with that, even my university degree that I really enjoyed, I can now remember little about. Turns out I was mostly using my shorter-term memory geared to pass the exams.

But there is another way, and through choosing to home educate three out of four of our children, my eyes have been opened to an alternative, more natural process of education.

With "unschooling," a type of home education where children follow their own self-directed learning, we move away from set curriculums and age-based targets. So this means children work on what they want to work on and how they want to work on it. Your child is a visual learner? Great! Your child is a hands-on learner? Also great!

Please note this is not the home schooling that you may have endured during the COVID-19 lockdown period. Forcing your children to sit at the kitchen table and complete work sent home from school whether or not they are interested to do it is not what we are talking about here. Unschooling is the antithesis to this!

Imperfection Alert: To follow the path of unschooling takes a lot of trust. Trust that children WILL learn what they need without having to be taught. It goes against everything we were taught ourselves as children—that we needed to learn whatever the teacher told us we needed to learn at that given point. Whether or not we were interested in it was irrelevant. Now was the time to learn it because the teacher told you so. Through traditional schooling, we experience that learning is something that happens TO you. With unschooling, we trust that learning is something that YOU do instinctively.

What if children could learn without being forced, just as they did when they learned to walk and to talk?

I am fortunate to have experienced three very different paths for my children learning to read that help me now stay true to the value of self-directed learning.

1) School taught—Emily attended school for a year and a term. She started school when she was four, along with all her little friends. I didn't feel right about her going to school, and I knew it wasn't just me as a mum feeling sad about her growing up and taking a step out of the nest. It was something fundamental, within me, it just didn't "feel right." But I didn't know about home education. So I sent her to school because, well, that's what everyone does.

   When Emily was at school, they started to teach her to read and she would come home with her early-reader books that we needed to complete, and very quickly we both fell out of love with this reading. The books, to allow for such a young brain, were very basic and mind-numbingly dull. The stories were created around the most basic phonic words that a four-year-old may be able to read, and as a result, the plot was somewhat lacking to say the least.

2) Early self-reader—With Alice, she actually taught herself to read at only age three. She just figured it out through a mixture of phonics and whole word learning. And one day I guess it just clicked. I didn't guide her. I only read stories to her as we usually would. And she just "did it." It was very exciting to see! And it gave me the confidence I needed to trust in the self-directed learning process.

3) More typical self-reader—With Florence, she is seven and she isn't reading fluently yet, but she is close. It has been fascinating to watch her journey. Alice's was so quick I didn't see the gradual building blocks her brain was making to be able to read. But with Florence, I have been able to witness the whole process in detail and it has been a privilege. I have enjoyed watching her start to recognise more and more words, so that sometimes she doesn't even realise that she has just pointed out a word to me. It's just a gradual natural progression. She is so close to being a fluent reader and I know she'll be fully ready when she is, as it has all come from her as her brain has naturally developed.

Out of the three different approaches to learning to read, both Alice and Florence love books. Emily doesn't. Now, maybe she wouldn't have loved books anyway, we'll never know. But I do wonder that if she'd been allowed to follow her own path and learned to read when she was ready, what a difference that would make to her reading enjoyment now.

Imperfection Tip: The beauty of self-directed learning—if you can learn to trust in the process—is that you never need to worry again. You don't need to compare your children to each other or to peers. Trust that your child is learning what they need to learn at just the time they need to learn it.

Another benefit of home education is that we socialise in mixed-age peer groups. In a school environment, children are placed within classes based on their age. But this isn't a natural way of being within society and can actually increase bullying and difficulties between children.

Think of your life as an adult now. Do you only socialise with people born within 12 months of you? Unlikely. One of my best friends is 11 years older than me, another is five years younger. What is important with friends is the bond you have, not the age you are.

For my children, socialising within mixed aged groups means they benefit from both older and younger ones. Older children to guide from their position of relative experience, younger children they themselves can help guide and nurture. When you see unschooled children socialising together, there are no tactics at play to exclude people, no teasing about someone being younger. I'm not pretending it's a utopia, but hand-on-heart I have never witnessed teasing or bullying at any unschooling meet up in all the years we have home educated. I think a reason for this is that these kids aren't fighting back against anything. For school children, who spend all day being told what to do, how to do it, and when to do it, when they get the freedom of their 15-minute playtime, they are often looking for ways to get some of their power back. And it is this that can sometimes get expressed in the form of bullying. The need to get some control.

I found for the short time that Emily was at school, her relationship with her sisters deteriorated as she was coming home and being mean to them, copying how some other children were being towards her in the playground, and attempting to make herself feel more in control again. Thankfully this all stopped when she left school, and as siblings they are extremely close now.

Imperfection Tip: Perhaps home education isn't for you. It is a big commitment to make and if you are used to the school system it can be a scary step to take. But if you have ever considered taking the leap, then I really urge you to consider it. It is a fantastic privilege to watch and witness my children's learning journeys. I love being by their side as they develop their knowledge and interests.

Imperfection Ideas:

\# What are the pros and cons of home education from your perspective? Make a list.

\# Are there ways to bring some of the positive elements of home education into your current life?

\# Find out about unschooling – perhaps follow some unschooling blogs on social media to learn more.

\# If you would like to try home education, what would you need to change in your life to make this a reality? Make a plan towards making those changes and take the first small step.

Respectful Parenting

Respectful parenting? Seriously? Kids need to earn respect! Once they show me respect, I'll show them respect! Eeek!

Be honest, do these sorts of thoughts ever go through your mind? For most of us, they do, as it is often how we ourselves were raised. But there is another way. At the very centre of respectful parenting is the principle that children are humans. Just as you and I as adults are human. And we are all born with the right to be treated with respect.

Respect isn't something you gain when you turn 18 or 21, it is an inherent right. Yet so often in our society we belittle children and treat them as less worthy because of their age. And yet we expect them to respect their elders? Their elders who are not treating them with respect? Hmm, really?? Why the double standards?

Children learn by watching what goes on around them. If you want to be treated with respect by your child, the most powerful way for them to learn that is to experience being treated with respect themselves.

Imperfection Tip: If you are finding this section triggering or uncomfortable, sit with those feelings for a while. What is coming up for you from your own childhood? Were you treated with respect? Did you ever feel forced to be a certain way? Did you ever feel like you didn't count?

What does respectful parenting look like in practical terms? Let's look at four different areas within my own family:

1) We have no set bedtimes—who am I to say when someone else is tired? It seems to me that most enforced bedtimes are for the parent's convenience rather than for the child. Of course children benefit from a certain amount of sleep, as we all do, but by helping a child understand their tiredness cues and how to encourage their bodies to sleep at appropriate times, your child will find their own routine. And you will be helping them establish good sleep practices for the rest of their lives.

2) Your body, your choice—body autonomy is really important to me. Don't force your children to hug or kiss someone they don't want to. I don't influence my children's clothes or hair choices—even when really young I would tell them what the weather would be before we went out, and I'd tell them if I was going to wear a coat for example, but I would not insist they did the same. Honour their autonomy over their own body. (And you can always bring them a coat in the car in case they change their mind).

3) You don't have to eat it—we meal plan together as a family now, but even when they were tiny, if they didn't like a food they didn't have to eat it. They might not even try it. There was no pressure. No rewards. No encouragement. No praise. Food is food. Eat the broccoli, don't eat the broccoli. I am not going to attach emotions to a piece of broccoli. I would say here as well that one of my children has a very restricted diet. But with our no pressure approach, I have noticed as she has grown older that she is starting to try more foods. Yay!

4) We are a no-rule household—seriously, we don't have rules. Do my children run amok? No. Do my children do whatever the heck they like? No. Instead of rules we talk about respect for others and for ourselves. My children aren't going to jump all over your sofas. They aren't going to come in and break all your kid's toys. They understand to treat others like they wish to be treated themselves. They

aren't perfect, just as you and I aren't perfect. And they make mistakes like we all do. But I don't need to control them with sets of rules to abide by with the threat of punishment for misdemeanours. If something happens that one of us is unhappy about, then we talk about it. From my experience, punishments only work to encourage secrecy and deviancy.

Imperfection Alert: Before I had children, I used to binge watch the TV show "Supernanny." You know, the one with the "naughty step" technique? I thought Supernanny was a miracle worker. And when I had my own children I did even use the naughty step technique for a little while with one of them. And then I read into it all a bit more and realised that it really isn't a good thing. The technique is meant to teach a child to reflect upon their actions, but the neo-cortex of a child's brain is not yet formed enough to do this. Instead, all the naughty step is doing is humiliating and excluding the child and encouraging them to internalise their emotions, because if they continue to "play up," they have to start all over again on their time on the step. You can do your own research, but I realised that for me this wasn't a technique I was happy to use, and I stopped. And we moved towards more respectful parenting, using connection and communication.

I tell you this, not to shame you if you use techniques like this, but to show you that it's ok to make mistakes and to change your mind over how you do something. And, most importantly, it is never too late to change your approach.

Imperfection Tip: Do the best you can until you know better, and when you know better, do better.

Ultimately, respectful parenting is about providing children with guidance rather than control and punishments. My children are not mine to control. They are their own beings. I respect them as such and help guide them when they need help. When you get to the essence, is that really so radical? It shouldn't be, and yet somehow, it has become so.

Respectful parenting will be harder to achieve if your children attend a nursery, preschool, or school setting. It is very hard to find settings where they do not use traditional child rearing practices of rewards and punishments. Rewards and punishments go against the grain of respectful parenting as you are ultimately rewarding children for behaving in a way that is acceptable to you and punishing them if they do not comply. Let's take an example as an adult. Pretend you came to my house for a cup of tea, and I offered you a biscuit. You said that you'd like one and went to take one. I then whisked the plate away and said, "What do you say? What's the magic word?" And then only if you said "please" would I pass you the biscuit. That seems ludicrous as an adult doesn't it? And actually rude. Yet we do that to children all the time, in the guise of teaching them "manners." Every day we ask for respect from children by treating them disrespectfully. Doesn't that seem a little odd?

It is possible for your children to attend outside-the-home settings and for you still to be a respectful parent, but usually it is a case of accepting that this is how your child will be dealt with while at that setting and just doing things differently at home. It would be good to explain to your children about the difference they'll experience and the reasons why as well, especially as they get older, as they'll be able to recognise that things work differently in different settings.

Imperfection Alert: When my youngest was in her final year at preschool, age three, we started to experience a problem. One of the assistants would frequently place her in time out/on the naughty step. It didn't happen with any other carers, just this one. I spoke to the manager of the preschool and explained the reasons why I didn't want them to use that sort of technique with my child, but I found out later that it did continue. And even now, at age seven, she talks about that assistant and her experiences of being singled out. I wish now I had followed up and made sure my child wasn't cared for by this person. Except for this incident, we have lovely memories of the preschool, but it shows how hard it can be to ensure true respect for your children in a more traditional setting.

Imperfection Ideas:

How did you feel when you were reading this section? If you felt uncomfortable about any of it take some time to

really consider what was going on for you.

Think back to when you were young? How were you treated? How did you feel? Are there any memories that come first to mind? (the ho'oponopono part in section three can help you here too).

Choose one area that causes conflict between you and your children – start with this area and commit to trying respectful parenting techniques instead. And keep trying! It is likely that you will sometimes revert to your old ways. When this happens, recognise it, and try again next time.

What would a no-rule household look like for you? What do the kids think? Order your list in an easiest-to-implement priority order. Choose the first step and bring in more autonomy for your children, then when that's established move on to the next step.

Living Seasonally

To live seasonally is something we have lost to a large extent in our modern lives. Our 24:7/365 world that means we are accessible all day every day, means we have also lost the innate natural rhythm of life. We still witness it (if we take care to notice) in the changes of the seasons and perhaps in the behaviour of animals. But we have forgotten that we too are part of this natural cycle. We don't experience it any longer. With every technological step, we have moved along one way, but we have also moved just a bit further away from our natural rhythm.

For us as a family, one of the key benefits of home working and home education means that time is our own. We can largely choose how to spend our days. We are not constrained by a timetable and expectations of an external body—be it the school or the workplace. And this means we can live more seasonally. Our natural rhythm really matches the seasons. During spring and summer months, we socialise more, we stay up late enjoying the lighter evenings, we are full of energy, and we respond to it. Come autumn and winter as the nights draw in, we slow down our pace of life. We have more lazy afternoons watching a movie and drinking hot chocolate. We see friends, but we have more down time because that is what we are drawn to at this time of year. We slow up our lifestyle.

Imperfection Alert: Last year we travelled around New Zealand for three months. We were there for their summer—which meant we missed our winter at home. And boy did I feel it when we got home! I don't regret going at all, but it made it even more clear to me how we really do need the down time that the colder seasons naturally allow for. I was "lucky" that it wasn't long after we came home that the UK went in to lockdown for COVID-19, so actually we ended up having the quiet winter hibernation months in the end, it was just enforced and during the springtime.

Imperfection Tip: How could you incorporate more

seasonality in your own life? Are there ways you could have more down time during colder months in order to recuperate and reenergise before the spring? Even something as simple as going to bed a bit earlier during the winter months can make a big difference to your energy levels once you emerge into the warmer months. If you need help to align your body to the naturally lower energy levels during the winter, consider setting aside a couple of evenings a week where you use candlelight only and have no TV or electronic screens. Your body will naturally tire earlier in line with the natural light levels as the evening draws in.

I find we instinctively do change what we eat in line with the seasons. More stew, curries, stodgy carbs during the colder months; more salad, lighter foods during the warmer months. Perhaps you find the same? This is your body's way of naturally reacting to the seasons. When you notice it and recognise it for what it is, you will find other ways present themselves to you where you can make changes and really embrace the natural cycle of life. Start to become more aware.

Imperfection Ideas:

What season are you in? What one change could you make to live more seasonally right now?

Plan ahead to the next season. What three changes can

you commit to make that will enable you to live more in line with the natural ebb and flow of the season.

Check in with yourself as the seasons change – can you recognise any changes within you as the light levels change and the natural energy levels alter.

Food and Drink

I am going to start at the most basic level. How much water do you drink? It is recommended to drink around two litres of water every day. Keeping properly hydrated boosts your energy levels and makes you more alert.

It's the most basic level of self-care, and it is where I would suggest you start if you are not already getting an adequate intake of water (and even if you think you are, actually measure it for a few days and check, what "feels" like enough water is often far short of the approximate two-litre target).

Imperfection Tip: Get yourself a bottle and measure out the water at the start of the day. And then make sure you drink it all before you go to bed. I have a one-litre bottle so I make sure I drink it and then refill it. A word of warning— when you first start this, you may feel like you are forcing yourself to drink far too much. And you will spend a lot of time on the toilet! But never fear, it is just your body adjusting to the intake. It will settle down and soon your body will be craving the water. For me, it only took a few days to adjust, though everyone is different, so do persevere.

Oh, and when I say water, I mean water. If you want your juice, or your coffee, that's fine, but that is in addition to the two-litres of water, not instead of! No cheating. Try it for a couple of weeks and see how much better you feel. It is best, if you can, to sip your water throughout the day, rather than chug down large quantities in one go. If you sip throughout the day then your body can use it as you need it. If you chug it down, much will just flush straight through and take some essential minerals and body salts on the way with it.

When you have the basic foundation of water sorted then you can start looking at your other habits around food and drink.

Sticking with drink for a bit longer. What about alcohol? How much are you drinking per week? This is a hard topic because alcohol is so rooted in our society and it is so normal to drink alcohol. A glass of wine every day is just an adult thing to do. Right? Nothing wrong with it, it's just a normal way to help us relax and to enjoy ourselves. And in a way, that's true. But equally, alcohol is a drug. Whatever your drink of choice, it is essentially ethanol dressed up in different ways. It is a drug like any other, just one that is acceptable in our society to consume, in a way that other drugs are not. We see alcohol as set apart somehow from all the other drugs, but essentially it is doing the same thing. Alcohol numbs the body and mind, easing stress temporarily and reducing inhibitions. Anyone that has ever had a stressful day and come home to a glass of wine or beer can attest to the de-stressing effect even from the first sip.

The problem comes, however, with the effect being only temporary. The stress relieved yesterday with a beer is still there when you wake up. And in truth, because alcohol alters the serotonin levels in your brain, it actually increases anxiety. So ultimately you'll feel worse. And it becomes a catch-22—you feel anxious so you relieve the feeling with a drink, the drink temporarily makes you feel better, but then ultimately makes you feel more anxious, so then you have another drink. Repeat. Repeat. Repeat.

Imperfection Alert: I was a regular drinker. From my late teens, through University, through my adult life all the way until my early forties. Except during my pregnancies, not many evenings passed by without a glass or two of wine. I certainly would never meet friends for an evening and not drink. That was unthinkable for me. But then in the back of my mind I always had the niggling thought that this wasn't a great thing to do. But then a glass or two of wine each night is ok, that's not alcoholic levels, it's just acceptable normal adult drinking levels. Isn't it? And yet this was the annoying doubt that just wouldn't quite be silenced. So on a whim I signed up to a 90-day no-alcohol challenge. And it was HARD. Breaking that daily habit was not an easy thing to do, and then there was the challenge of meeting friends for evening drinks, or going to parties, or going on holiday—all the times I usually associated with alcohol and suddenly needed to do completely sober.

But I persevered, and it got a bit easier, and then after probably around the two-month mark, something changed. Something clicked in my brain. I realised how good I felt. I was sleeping deep, uninterrupted sleep (except when the children woke me!). I was waking earlier, with energy. I was more patient in the daytime with my children. I just felt energised and happy. And it was then I realised what alcohol was robbing me of. The alcohol I had thought was enabling me to enjoy life was actually the thing that was stopping me being able to fully enjoy life in the first place.

And so I haven't had a drink since, around a year and a half now. Which is just amazing, and I cannot believe that I am a non-drinker. If you had told me that two years ago I would never, never have believed you.

It's quite hard to write this section as I know how I would have read it when I was drinking, telling myself I don't have a drinking problem. There is nothing wrong with a beer or a glass of wine on an evening. That going out and sharing a bottle of wine was fundamental to my socialising. Drink was an enjoyable thing to do and it enhanced my life. And that may be how you feel too. But if you are honest with yourself, I wonder if there is any niggle of self-doubt lurking there. Because I had that. I ignored it for many years, but it was there. And if you do have that niggle of doubt then just start to listen to it. You may not be ready to stop drinking entirely, but perhaps you could cut down from what you currently drink? I started by attempting to moderate and having certain days I didn't drink. For me the problem was that it just made me focus all the more on my drinking days, I was only enduring the non-drinking times. But it was a step in the right direction and ultimately led me towards the challenge, which in the end extended from 90 days to (I hope) the rest of my life.

Imperfection Tip: If you want to cut out or cut down on alcohol, then alcohol-free substitutes can really help make the transition easier. There are plenty of lager, cider, gin, and wine alternatives. They are not hugely healthy, but they help minimise the cravings in the early days that your body will be shouting about around the time it would usually be expecting that alcoholic drink.

Enough about drink. What about food? Don't worry. I'm not about to tell you I cut out chocolate too. I wish I could cut out refined sugars, but I am not there yet! What I want to focus on is overall looking at what you put into your body and also the environmental impact of the food we eat. The big one has to be meat. Whether you believe we were born to eat meat or not, the fact is that the way we produce the meat is hugely damaging to the environment. The statistics you can find will vary, but agriculture consistently comes out as one of the top industries causing harm to the environment through greenhouse gas emissions. It is partly the emissions from the animals themselves (particularly cows), but also the clearing of land for agriculture, particularly to grow feed for the animals. It is a huge problem.

What can you do? Going vegan or even vegetarian is the biggest individual change you could make. But for many that is not a comfortable change to consider. If you fall into this latter camp, then why not consider having fewer meals without meat each week? Perhaps you could be meat-free during the weekdays? Any reduction in the amount of meat you consume will have an impact. There are meat-substitutes readily available to make simple swaps, though these are not always the healthiest choice and can be expensive, but they can make the transition to eating less meat that much easier. Or you may enjoy trying different styles of food entirely rather than attempting to fake your usual meat meals. See what works best for you, and remember it's all about the small steps.

Imperfection Ideas:

\# Drink two litres of water today. And then tomorrow. And then for the rest of the week….month….

\# Think about how much alcohol you are currently drinking. When are you consuming it (at home? When you go out?) and most importantly, WHY. You need to dig deep and be honest with yourself.

\# With this information are there any changes you want to make? If there are, put in place one commitment to implement and stick with it for three months.

Commit to two meat-free days per week.

Eating Seasonally

I talked earlier about matching our lifestyle and routines around the natural energy levels of the seasons. But what about the food you are eating? We have become so used to the global food culture and finding whatever food we want, whenever we want it, I think a lot of people have forgotten that foods even have a season.

Imperfection Alert: I was sixteen years old when I realised that apples had a season. And all other fruit and vegetables too! I really did not know until then. The fact was that I had grown up in a culture where we could buy strawberries if we wanted strawberries, or apples if we wanted apples, and so on. The time of year was irrelevant. I didn't see any evidence to suggest that these foods weren't naturally available in my country all year round. The truth that we ship food around the globe to satisfy our year-round demand for what should be seasonal products, had until that point, passed me by. And I am sure I won't be the only child, or even adult, that hasn't realised that.

I do think we are now so used to eating a wide variety of food throughout the year that for most people it would not be realistic to achieve wholly seasonal eating. However, we can all make small changes.

Imperfection Tip: Eat more of what is in season—growing your own really helps here as you see it grow, and then you pick it to eat. The seasonality of what you grow is clear. Buying food in the supermarkets requires a bit more effort and knowledge about what grows when and where. But it is possible, it just takes some thought. And the truth is, nothing tastes better than locally grown fruit and veg that is in season.

Imperfection Ideas:

Find out what fruit and vegetables are in season right now where you live.

Commit to buying more of the in-season produce and reduce your out-of-season produce.

Research recipes and arrange to have one totally in-season meal every week.

Caffeine and Other Stimulants

How do you start the day? With a cup of coffee or tea most likely? I get it, I love my morning cup of tea too. Never got into coffee I must admit, it must be the British-ness in me, but tea—now that hits the spot. And there are lots of health benefits so we're told from a good old cuppa (antioxidants mainly). The thing that isn't so great however is the caffeine. Caffeine is a stimulant. Or in more stark language, a drug. It raises our heart rate and blood pressure, and this is why it helps us feel more alert. The problem is it is only the effect of the caffeine making us feel this way. We are not REALLY feeling more alert, we just think that we are. And then when the effects of the caffeine start to wear off and we feel less alert again, we start looking for our next hit. Caffeine in low doses is regarded as safe, I am not here to scaremonger, but there are certainly better, more natural ways to increase your energy levels—check out some of the ideas in Section Three. What concerns me is that, like any drug, our bodies enjoy the experience and demand more. And before we know it, we are consuming quite a lot of caffeine to create the effect of alertness that we want, but we are masking the fact that we are lacking the alertness in the first place. Does that make sense? We shouldn't need artificial drugs or stimulants to make us feel a certain way.

Reducing our reliance on stimulants such as caffeine can really only be a good thing. When you strip out stimulants from your body, you can then start to properly tune in to your body's needs. What is your body's natural rhythm?

Imperfection Tip: Consider how much caffeine you are currently consuming in a day (don't forget some fizzy drinks also contain caffeine). Could you cut down from that? Maybe start by cutting out the fizzy drinks, or removing one or two cups of coffee. Just make a start. Or if you are really brave, you could go cold turkey! Just be aware, that however you go about it, when you try to cut out or cut down on caffeine, your body will have something to say about it. Expect it to shout. Loudly. Think of your body rather like a child with a bag of sweets. How loudly will the child scream if you try to take away the sweets? So prepare yourself. But after a couple of days, your body will begin to adjust; it won't take long, but it does take perseverance. As with any drug, your brain will continue to crave it for quite a while. So this isn't for the faint hearted, but it is a change you can make that you will very quickly feel the benefits from. And there are lots of decaffeinated coffees and teas on the market, so you can keep the taste of your favourite drink without having to have the artificial stimulation that usually comes along with it.

Imperfection Alert: I used to have a Coke habit. As in Coca-Cola. I was a one-can-a-day girl for many years. Not interested in the diet stuff, I am talking full-sugar, full-hit, red-can stuff. I fell into my habit when I was working in an office and it gave me a boost at lunchtime. And then I didn't drink it during pregnancy, but when the children were little, I slipped back in to my one-a-day habit as a way to boost me on through the afternoon. I was sleeping very poorly due to getting up with children throughout the night, and it was the hit of "energy" I needed to see me through the afternoon (before I would get my hit of "calm" on an evening through my glass of wine). But I knew it wasn't good for me (and ironically, of course, if I hadn't been drinking the Coke and the wine, my sleep would have been better quality too).

I was drinking decaffeinated tea but didn't acknowledge the white elephant in the room in the form of the shiny red-can packaging. Eventually though, I think spurred by the fact that the children were growing older and more interested in what I was consuming, I decided enough was enough. And so I stopped. And it was hard. SO hard. And I relapsed a fair few times. But I persevered. And now I don't drink it. Well, not never, I occasionally (maybe three times a year) will have a can. But it isn't often. And I don't let myself get drawn down that slippery slope. I know when I do have one I will crave one the day after at around the same time, but if I can ride through that craving, then it goes away and I don't get it again the day after that.

You don't have to go as far as me and abstain completely. But just be mindful of what you are putting into your body and why you are doing it. If you are looking for an energy fix then question why you are lacking in energy. What else could you do to raise your vibe? Now, if I am feeling lethargic after lunch, I put on some music and dance or have a good sing-along in the car. There are many ways to get your energy kicked back up to where you need it without having to use caffeine or other stimulants.

Imperfection Ideas:

\# Work out how much caffeine you consume during an average day.

Buy a caffeine-free alternative for your tea or coffee, replace one cup a day with your decaf product.

Have one caffeine-free day a week.

Cook from Scratch

How many ready meals and take outs do you get each week? And by ready meals, I mean any pre-prepared processed food. Pasta sauces? Jars of curry sauces? Tins of baked beans?

These products exist to make our lives easier. And they do save us time. But what they also do is remove us from the knowledge of what is in the food that we are putting into our bodies. As an example, think of corn flakes. It's an easy breakfast option and viewed as a healthy alternative to many other cereals, which may be full of refined sugar. But did you know that your standard bowl of corn flakes could have as much salt in them as a bag of ready-salted crisps? Unless you specifically check, and really, why would you ever think that corn flakes would have so much salt, then you just don't know.

When you cook from scratch, you know exactly what goes into your food. You know about the teaspoon of sugar you added to sweeten your tomato sauce. You know about the salt you added to your casserole to help the flavour. And the good news is that cooking from scratch can be really cheap—cheaper than pre-prepared alternatives anyhow. Not always, but usually. To really reduce your costs, I find that meal planning is the best way to save money on your shopping; by pre-planning you only buy exactly what you need and not all the extra bits and pieces that increase your spending. So once a week, sit down and plan out a week's worth of meals.

Imperfection Tip: Perhaps a whole week of cooking from scratch is too much? Why not start with once or twice a week? Or you could batch cook some dishes one day and freeze them, then you have the meals all ready for when you need them through the week—homemade ready meals!

Imperfection Alert: I was spending a lot of money on food at the supermarket yet we never seemed to have much food in the house. I fought against meal planning for a long time as it just felt so restrictive. I don't want to think about what I am doing tomorrow until tomorrow. But I tried it because I was told I could save a lot of money. And in making the change, I halved our shopping bill! Once a week we plan out what we will cook (everyone in the family is in charge of at least one meal a week, though when I started it was just me doing the cooking), we buy the required food, and then we know who is cooking what, when. I thought I would find it restrictive, but I actually find it liberating. I no longer have to think every day about what we will have for dinner, because it's already planned out. So I know that we are having vegetable lasagne or whatever it is, and if it's my turn to cook or if I'll need to help anyone with their cooking, and I don't have to be using my brain power and energy to think any more about it.

And cooking from scratch doesn't have to take a long time. Pasta and homemade sauce could take just ten minutes for example. And as I mentioned, you could also batch prepare meals all on one day and freeze them, then all you need to do is reheat them when you want to eat.

And it isn't just main meals. What are you snacking on? Are there home-alternatives you could prepare for yourself?

Imperfection Alert: Let me give you a real example from our household. The kids were getting through a lot of yoghurt, and it was a go-to snack very often as yoghurt is healthy, right? Hmm, not necessarily. Did you know that many shop-bought yoghurts have around half of your total recommended amount of sugar in them? In just that one little pot! Some yoghurts have the same amount of sugar in them as a chocolate bar. Those yoghurts that look really deliciously healthy with all the fruit at the bottom are some of the worst culprits. Plus of course, we have the packaging issue with all those one-use tubs and cartons. So I stopped buying yoghurt and we just ate loads of chocolate instead. Joke! I stopped buying the shop-bought yoghurt and I started buying a big tub of natural Greek yoghurt, I then make a fruit compote, which I sweeten with a natural sweetener (I use agave syrup or maple syrup), and we can sweeten it to our own taste and know how much is in there. When we want yoghurt, we just mix some of the compote in a bowl with some of the natural yoghurt. And the compote lasts for ages in an air-tight container.

Moving from pre-prepared shop bought products to making your own can feel daunting, but it really doesn't have to be. As I said, I have found planning out meals not only saved me money, but has also saved my brain power from having to think each day about what to cook. And you don't need to switch out everything, remember, start with the small steps!

Imperfection Ideas:

Think about an average week – how often are you eating pre-prepared foods?

Swap out one pre-prepared food that you commit to not buy again, and replace with a homemade alternative.

Research recipes to cook from scratch twice a week.

Meal plan for two weeks – see how much money you can save, and you'll reduce food waste too!

Good Sleep Practices

We all know we need sleep, and we all know how much better we feel when we get enough rest. Sleep allows our mind and body to repair itself, and regular poor sleep even reduces our life expectancy. Yikes! But if it is so important to us, why is it sometimes so darn difficult to get a good night's sleep?!

If you have children waking you up during the night then that is one thing, and this is something you cannot battle against. I feel for you. I have been there. I am still there. My eldest daughter at the age of 10, still—and I am guessing, probably always will—wakes most nights. But even if this is your situation, there are still things you can control to make sure that what sleep you do get is the best sleep available to you.

1. Do some exercise earlier in the day or early evening. This helps relieve the stresses and tension of the day (see Section Three for some ideas around this) from your mind and your body.

2. Stay off the alcohol. I know it feels like you need that beer or glass of wine to help get you to sleep, but the reality is that it makes the quality of your sleep pretty poor. Alcohol reduces, or even blocks, your REM (rapid eye movement) sleep, which is your most restorative period of sleep. And stay away from other stimulants like caffeine too. With any of these things you are just disrupting your

natural circadian rhythms and your body's ability to recognise and respond to sleep cues.

3. Step away from your phone. If the last thing you are doing at night is checking your Facebook feed, then this isn't helping your body or mind prepare for sleep. By using devices such as tablets or smartphones (and even TV) before bed, you are disrupting your body's ability to release melatonin, which is the natural hormone we kick out around our body to tell ourselves to go to sleep. The blue light on these devices tell our minds that it is daytime and keeps us more alert, plus your brain is engaging with the content of whatever is on your screen instead of becoming restful for sleep. So keep your phone out of your bedroom if you want a good night's sleep!

4. Establish a routine. Try to go to bed around the same time every night. And factor in enough downtime once you are in bed. When your life is on the go all day, it isn't realistic to think you can hop into bed and go straight to sleep without some sort of transition.

5. And you need to plan for this transition. Now is a good time to do some gratitude work (see Section Three) and/or journaling. This acts as a way to change your brain patterns from the busy day time to the quieter night time. When you are lying in

bed, it isn't a great time to meditate as you need to stay awake during meditation, however, it is a good time for slow, deep breathing and generally slowing your mind down, and meditative techniques can help you with this.

Imperfection Alert: I sleep with my phone by my bed. It's not great I know, but there it is. And I look at it when I am in bed, BUT I limit myself to fifteen minutes and then I switch if off and put it on airplane mode. And then I read. I read usually for around half an hour—this seems to be the time when my brain will start feeling sleepy. At that point, I turn off the light and think of three things I feel grateful for (see more in Section Three), and then those are my final thoughts as I drift off to sleep.

Imperfection Tip: Set aside some time as an active bedtime routine—sleep should come naturally but it can be hard to still your whirring mind so actively taking steps to calm your senses can help. Try journaling, or reading, or deep breathing. Or maybe a combination. See what works for you. And then when you start to feel sleepy, act on it; don't decide to read just a little bit longer or to write just a few more points in your journal. Switch off the light and catch the sleepy wave before it goes. When I miss the wave, it can be another fifteen minutes or more before it comes around again, and when it does, it is never quite as perfect as the first wave that came.

Imperfection Ideas:

\# Think about your current sleep routine. How much sleep are you getting every night? How do you feel when you wake up?

\# Make one change today to improve your sleep routine.

\# Remove your phone from your bedroom (this one is for me as much as you!).

Celebrate Nature

There are key times throughout the year where it is nice (and good for us) to pause, to consider, to notice, and to be thankful of the natural rhythms within nature. The pagans were really good at this, as were the Celts, and actually most ancient cultures. To my mind, there is no conflict to find ways to celebrate these times in nature, as well as hold true to any other religion you may practice, but as with anything, look inside yourself and see what feels comfortable to you. If you are interested in celebrating some key times in nature's calendar then these are some to be getting on with (note I haven't given specific dates as this will depend on whether you live in the northern or southern hemisphere so research further as appropriate):

- **Yule (winter solstice)**—The shortest day/longest night of the year. We are in the depths of winter at this point, and if we are observing our natural rhythms, we'll tend to have less energy, feel less sociable, and be spending more time indoors. It is a good time for stillness and for introspection; to consider how the past year has been, and what we might want to do differently in the coming year.

Celebration Idea: Celebrate by decorating your house with evergreens, light a fire and maybe some candles. Sit around the fire—on your own or with a group—and on a piece of paper write down the things that you would like to let go of. What no longer serves you? Throw this paper on the fire and feel the release of energy as the paper burns. Visualise all that you had written leaving your body forever. And then take the time to welcome in new traits to the energy space you have cleared. How do you want to be in the coming year? What are you going to do differently? As you watch the fire burn, fill your body with positive energy, knowing that from this solstice the days will get longer and the positive energy within you and around you will grow.

- **Imbolc**—Translates as "in the belly of the mother." Imbolc is about celebrating the early stirrings of new growth from mother earth. It is a time about halfway between the winter solstice and the spring equinox. You may notice buds starting to push their way out of the earth for the beginnings of spring, nature seems to be coming back to life giving us all new hope and positive energy.

Celebration Idea: Nuts and seeds are symbolic of new growth so it is nice to incorporate these into an Imbolc celebration. Come together with family or friends to bake a loaf of bread from scratch. Share the mixing and the kneading, and each add in a handful of nuts and seeds to the dough. Consider lighting candles and maybe some purifying herbs or essential oils, and eat the bread together while sharing your hopes for your own new growth.

- **Ostara (spring equinox)**—This is the first time of year when the day and night is the same length, and it is recognised as the first day of spring. This time is about fertility and hopefulness. You will notice the spring flowers around you and the buds growing on the trees. Energy levels are strong and you may feel that anything is possible if you set your mind to it.

Celebration Idea: Eggs are a sign of fertility so decorating eggs at this time of year is a nice thing to do, and something many people may already do as part of Easter. It can also be nice to take some time on your own or with others out in nature. Find a tree to sit under and be still. Notice what you can see, what you can hear. Feel the energy from the ground rise up through your body, as, at the same time, the energy from your body roots down into the ground. Take the time to feel at one with the nature that we are part of.

- **Beltane (May day)** —Energy is high, flowers are in bloom, trees have blossomed. The earth feels alive (because, let's not forget of course, it is) and positivity fills the air. This is a time when things are growing and we witness the combined power of the sun and the earth.

Celebration Idea: Plant some seeds, tend to them, and watch them grow. Choose vegetable seeds that you can grow, nurture, and then eat, as a way to become a direct part of nature's growing cycle. You could also light a fire and dance around it to celebrate the energy that is burning within and around you at this time of year.

- **Litha (summer solstice)**—The longest day/shortest night of the year. This is a time of high energy! However, while it is a time of our highest energy, it is also the start of the waning of nature's energy, as the nights begin to lengthen from this point onwards. This is our time to celebrate the sun and the energy it gives us.

Celebration Idea: Watch the sun rise, spend the day outside in nature, and then watch the sun set. Feel the energy of the sun's cycle from the first glimpses in the morning through the heat of the midday, all the way to the last warm touches at night. Be present and be thankful. Knowing that energy from this time will start to ebb, now is a good point to check in on your intentions you set at the winter solstice and make sure you are on the path that you want to be for the remainder of the year.

- **Mabon (autumn equinox)**—The second equinox of the year, where the day and night are of equal length. A time of balance. Around us the leaves are beginning to turn autumnal and we know that winter isn't far away. This is a last chance to consider what you want to achieve before the lower winter energy. The harvest means that food is abundant, and now is a good time to celebrate this abundance.

Celebration Idea: Share a harvest feast with family or friends. Cook from scratch using foods locally in season. Celebrate all that nature has provided. You could also take the time together to plant some spring bulbs in preparation for the coming year.

- **Samhain (all hallows eve/Halloween)**—This is the time of year where it is said that we are closest to the spirit world. In Mexico, they celebrate the Dia de Muertos (Day of the Dead) where they remember and honour their deceased ancestors. You'll probably be aware of the more modern western traditions based around dressing up and collecting sweets from neighbours, but this can be a time for more spiritual observation if you want it to be.

Celebration Idea: Walk in nature and marvel at the autumn colours and the dying-off of the natural life. Light a fire outside, or be at home with candles, and take the time to remember ancestors and recognise the energy they left behind that is now within you. Celebrate all they have given you and all that, in time, you will pass on.

Imperfection Ideas:

\# Commit to celebrate whichever natural celebration is next on the calendar.

\# Look at your usual year. What celebrations and traditions do you already take part in? Is there an obvious gap in your celebrations calendar where you could add a new tradition?

\# Mark on your calendar all the natural celebration times.

- - Summary - -

These lifestyle changes in Section Two may take deeper thought than our "household" changes in Section One, but these changes are still within your easy reach. The important thing is to make a commitment. And remember, to start you only have to take one small step. Starting with committing to drink two litres of water a day is a step towards being more mindful about what you put in to your body; removing your smartphone from your bedroom at night time is a step towards prioritising better sleep; noticing how you speak to your children and what you demand of them is a step towards respectful parenting. You don't have to make the big changes until you feel ready, just take one step in the direction you wish to head.

SECTION THREE: WELL-BEING

In this section, we are looking at changes you can make to your daily life that will enable you to align your mind and your body to live in a more natural state of being. This is our most holistic section, and we will look at everything from spending time outside in nature, to meditation, through to the benefit of exercise. We will look at how to build in daily routines to care for your body and your mind.

We will be talking about feel-good hormones that your body produces naturally and ways you can boost the production of these chemicals. I'll outline here the main hormones we'll be looking at:

- **Endorphins**—produced by the pituitary gland and central nervous system. They are chemicals that are released into our bodies to relieve pain and to make us feel good. The release of endorphins into our bodies is said to have a similar effect to morphine (just without all the side effects!).

- **Serotonin**—the mood regulator. Serotonin boosts our feelings of well-being and happiness. Serotonin can help lower depression and anxiety, and it also plays an important part in healthy digestion.

- **Oxytocin**—the love hormone. It plays a particularly important role in female reproduction; it gets released in huge quantities during and after childbirth and helps encourage bonding between the mother and the baby. However, it's not just for birthing mothers. Oxytocin plays an important role for all social bonding; it is a feel-good hormone. It is released for both men and women during orgasm, and for men it helps in the movement of sperm. Low oxytocin levels have been linked to depression.

- **Dopamine**—the pleasure hormone. Works as part of your brain's reward system. Dopamine is released during pleasurable experiences, acting as a reward for seeking those experiences and encouraging you to seek them again. Dopamine is released during sex, also when drinking alcohol or taking drugs, or when eating food that we crave. Dopamine is a big player in anticipatory pleasure and works to motivate you. If you find you are lacking in enthusiasm, and you frequently feel apathy and often rely on stimulants to get through the day (tea/coffee/sugar/alcohol, etc.), then you may well be low on dopamine.

The following section looks at what we can do to boost our natural levels of these mood-enhancing hormones.

And while we are touching upon the science, I want to briefly discuss the vagus nerve, which is fundamental to our well-being and can be strengthened through many of the areas I discuss in this section.

- **What is the vagus nerve? Why is it important?**

The vagus nerve is the longest nerve within the autonomic nervous system, which means it works without us having to control it; it is a key part of the parasympathetic nervous system and controls many of our major organs and digestive system. *Vagus* in Latin means wanderer, and the vagus nerve is sometimes known as the wandering nerve, which is a good description of the way it is linked to so many areas of our bodies.

Having a toned vagus nerve means your body is better able to regulate itself. The vagus nerve triggers our natural fight, flight, freeze response (and our ability to come down again after being triggered); a person with a strong vagus nerve is able to relax more quickly again following stress. A person with an undertoned vagus nerve is more susceptible to depression, stress, and various health conditions such as arthritis, diabetes, chronic inflammation, and cardiovascular disease.

It is not possible to tone the vagus nerve directly (well, not without an implanted device), but by working on areas of your body that the vagus nerve is linked to will help tone your vagus nerve and enable the well-being for your body and your mind that you are seeking. Activities such as meditation, deep breathing, singing, fasting, and cold showers can all help. We'll cover these and more as we work through this section.

Exercise

I know, I know. But just hear me out. The thing is, it is actually really good for us. Believe me, if it wasn't I'd be the first to say let's not bother. But the fact is, we need it. Our bodies need it and our minds need it. When we exercise, we release endorphins that make us feel good, and in particular, regular exercise raises our levels of serotonin, which boosts our mood and sense of well-being. Sounds pretty good, eh?

So the first step is to acknowledge that this exercise thing could be worth a try. Then you need to work out what exercise could look like for you. Now, many people, so I hear, love nothing more than to pull on some shiny leggings and a pair of trainers, and start pounding the streets for miles at a time. If that's you, then great! Go for it. But, that might not be where you are at. The good news is that exercise doesn't have to look like exercise. What about a dance class? A swim? Don't want to leave the house? No problem, do an online HIIT (high intensity interval training) session. There is something for everyone.

Imperfection Tip: The best type of exercise for boosting endorphins is cardiovascular exercise (i.e., anything that gets the heart rate raised).

Imperfection Alert: I have never been a regular exerciser. I have done a bit of running. I enjoyed Zumba classes for a while. I have been known (pre-children) to have a gym membership. I even used it. Occasionally. But, like all my attempts at exercise, once the novelty wears off, I can come up with a million and one excuses not to do it anymore. However, at the start of the lockdown period for coronavirus, I found out about Joe Wicks, aka The Body Coach, and his "PE with Joe" initiative. I did every 30-minute workout Monday to Friday over the 18 weeks or so that he ran the sessions. And I have since continued with three-times a week HIIT sessions, using repeated episodes and other sessions from his channel. For me it works as I don't need to fit it in around the children—they can even join in should they wish! I can wear whatever I like. No one sees me. And … it's actually quite fun. I certainly feel so much better for having done the session, and that feel-good feeling stays with me all day—all that lovely serotonin doing its thing.

The important thing is just to try something and to stick with it for a while. How do you feel before you start a session? And how do you feel at the end of the session? Do you feel better, more positive? Do something at least three times a week, commit to it, and after a month see how you feel. If you have more energy and feel more positive then this will knock over into the rest of your life.

Imperfection Tip: Make a note of what exercise you do and rate your mood each time pre-workout and post-workout. You'll be able to monitor what is having an impact on you over time. Also, identify if different types of exercise work better for you at different points of the month or at different times of the day.

Remember, if other commitments make it difficult to leave the house to attend a class then look at what you can find online. Honestly, I didn't know until recently that there was so much available. And so much of it is free! Just remember to take it carefully, and if you have pre-existing conditions, speak to your doctor first before trying anything new.

Imperfection Ideas:

\# What exercise do you currently do? What exercise do you enjoy?

\# Research online exercise options. Is there something you could try?

\# Commit to doing one form of exercise once a week for half an hour. Then increase it to two times a week. And then three.

Yoga

I have been a long-time advocate of yoga. It is so beneficial for your body and mind. But to be truthful, I haven't always done a regular yoga practice. With four young children at home, it was just too difficult to find the time to attend a class (or more accurately, I had an easy excuse not to find the time). But, again, here is where the coronavirus lockdown actually helped me. I discovered online yoga sessions on YouTube. Where have I been, right? But they have changed my life. One of my daughters is an early riser, so when she and I are up on a morning, she sits and watches her iPad at one end of the room, I unroll my yoga mat at the other end and choose a session. Sometimes if I am short on time I may only do a ten-minute session. But I always do something, and it sets me up for the day.

Imperfection Alert: Since turning forty, my body seems to be ceasing up. I have always been super-duper flexible and I guess I just took it for granted. And then wham! Forty came and turned off my stretchy superpowers. Just like that. Gone. But through my regular yoga practice, I am noticing some of my stretchability (I may have made up that word) coming back. And when I am feeling frustrated with it or unmotivated to practice, I think of my next-door neighbour. She is 85, regularly practices yoga, and can even do a tripod headstand pose (sirsasana). She puts my creaky version of downward dog to shame.

Imperfection Tip: The benefit of the online yoga sessions is there is no one else there to see that you can't reach your toes, and you don't have the distraction of wondering whether the lady in front of you knows that her leggings are not squat proof ... your mind can stay focused on the yoga positions and transitions without worrying what is going on around you. And if you have children at home, you can do it at any time of the day without being restricted to a class schedule. Saying that, I do feel there is additional value from attending classes in person in terms of ensuring proper positioning, plus, attending a class alongside others can give your oxytocin an extra kick too. So one day I will get back to a class practice, but for now, online is suiting me better.

Yoga is good for both your body and your mind; it is a natural serotonin booster. I mentioned how yoga has helped me with my flexibility but regular practice also improves your health and strength, and can help reduce symptoms of depression, anxiety, and stress. And the regulated breathing techniques that yoga practices encourage (pranayama) help tone your vagus nerve. Yoga has been around for somewhere between five to 10,000 years; our ancestors knew the benefits, now it's your turn to try it.

Imperfection Tip: All still sounds a bit too energetic? Try Yoga Nidra (or yogic sleep). It is a deep-relaxation yoga practice, which is not only one of the most relaxing things you will ever experience, but it also raises your dopamine levels. Try a class, I promise you will thank me.

Imperfection Ideas:

\# Try a yoga class – online or out of the house

\# Look at different types of yoga, can you try a new practice?

\# Commit to practicing yoga once a week – and increase it to three times a week when you are able.

\# Start every day with a ten minute yoga stretch. Find an online session to guide you.

Meditation

Or mindfulness if you prefer. Similar with my exercise and yoga routines, I have been more of a toe dipper into the world of meditation, never a regular practitioner. However, relatively recently I started getting up early every day to create the time to do it. In our daily lives, we are surrounded by stimulus and immersed in busyness. Our brains are dominated by constant thoughts. Mine go something like this ... I need to get Sophie a birthday card this week—I should have vacuumed the lounge at the weekend—I must remember to take a toilet roll upstairs—oooo I wonder what bird that was in the garden—what shall I make for dinner tonight?—I need to decide what colour we should paint the bathroom—I wonder if the jeans I want are in stock yet online (pick up phone to check and instead automatically open Facebook)—(ten minutes of mindless scrolling later)—What did I pick my phone up for? ... And so it goes on. And on. And on. And it never stops.

But with meditation it can stop. For a little bit. You can start to have control over your thought processes and pause the chatter. The constant internal chat is where our brains are operating at a beta level. With meditation, we remove ourselves from the drain of thoughts, sinking our brains to an alpha level where our minds find more stillness and we can start to access our subconscious, which is what drives 95 percent of our brain. Seriously, 95 percent of our decisions actually come from the subconscious brain, only five percent from the conscious brain. So to make changes in your life, you need to make friends with your subconscious. How does this work?

Say you decide that you want to attract more money into your life. That would be nice, right? So your conscious brain has the thought "Yes I want to attract more money in to my life." Excellent. And your conscious brain keeps thinking these thoughts. It keeps you on track, focusing on all the brilliant things you will do when you have more money. But in the background, it is your subconscious brain that is really driving the decisions. So if your subconscious brain has stories around money—for example, that to have a lot of money you need to work really hard, or maybe it believes that rich people aren't nice—if it believes any stories like this then your subconscious brain is going to do everything it can to stop you achieving your goal. Your subconscious exists to keep you safe, and if you have internal stories that mean it is not safe for you to have more money (e.g., that you'll have to work all the time, or that people won't like you anymore) then your subconscious will work away to ensure it doesn't happen.

The good news is that we can rewire our brains. Meditation allows you to still your conscious mind and start to notice what is going on deeper within you at your subconscious level. Once you work through these with meditation, you can reprogramme your subconscious brain and get it on board with the choices you want to make. Until you do, you'll be stuck in your current reality whether you like it or not.

Imperfection Tip: Meditation is hard. I'm not going to beat around the bush here. It really is hard. Sitting there attempting to still your conscious brain takes work. And this is something you will need to work at. To start with, try a daily practice of maybe ten to twenty minutes every day. It is only with repeated practice that you will make progress. Like any exercise, you need to work at it and build up.

Meditation has been found to improve our attention levels, reduce stress, improve mental health, help preserve our brains as we grow older, improve learning and memory function, and it reduces anxiety. And that list isn't exhaustive. Meditation also helps strengthen our vagus nerve.

I would certainly say it's worth a try to see what benefits it can bring into your life. Wondering how long to meditate for? We'll finish with this old Zen saying:

"You should sit in meditation for twenty minutes every day—unless you're too busy. Then you should sit for an hour."

Imperfection Ideas:

Set aside ten minutes every day to meditate. Decide on a time of day and stick to it, every day, for a week.

When you have meditated consistently for one week, look to extend it to two, and then a month. You could also extend the time you are spending in meditation. For me, the longer periods bring the most benefit.

Use meditative techniques to pause during your day. Set aside key times or trigger points within your day – it could be after every meal, or maybe when you start to feel cross. Allow yourself a couple of minutes of deep breathing to check in with yourself.

Ho'oponopono

This a really useful practice for clearing out thoughts, regrets, and blocks in your life. Are there areas in your life where you feel stuck, or do you have memories that keep coming back to you that you just can't shake off? With ho'oponopono you revisit your memories and release them, using a simple but effective mantra: I'm sorry. I forgive you. Thank you. I love you.

Imperfection Tip: Spend some time writing down whatever comes to mind. You could start with your earliest memories and work up to age seven as a starting point, or whatever makes sense for you. Just write down whatever comes to mind—you may be surprised at what comes up. Don't fight it, just accept the memories into your consciousness and write them down. Then when you have written down everything that you need to, take your first memory that you wrote down, close your eyes, and think back to that memory. And then you repeat the important mantra. You can say the mantra in whatever order you wish; I say it "I'm sorry. I forgive you. Thank you. I love you."

So, as an example, say you are thinking back to a time when you were little, you broke a cup and were shouted at by your mum or dad. Remember the event and how you felt. And then you think through the mantra:

I'm sorry—to your little self for being shouted at for an accident.

I forgive you—to your little self for breaking the cup, and, if you want, to the person that shouted at you.

Thank you—for forgiving myself now and letting go of the memory. Thank you for the incident in helping make me the strong person I am today.

I love you—to yourself as the little child and to you now, and, if you want, to the person that shouted at you.

You can say the words out loud if you want, I just do it in my head. And then you can also score through that memory on your paper as a physical sign that you have dealt with the memory. And then you move on to the next one on your list.

You can then repeat this process another time for later memories, or also for specific memories that seem to play on your mind, or if you feel you have certain emotional blocks. And it's always worth repeating the exercise. Some memories will come up for you more than once. But in time you will clear the memories that are holding you back and free up your energy to make new and exciting changes in your life.

Imperfection Ideas:

Set aside half an hour to try ho'oponopono. Spend ten to fifteen minutes writing out memories that come to mind (don't censor them). Then spend fifteen minutes working through them using ho'oponopono.

Commit to spending thirty minutes every week on ho'oponopono, try it for a month.

Practice Gratitude

This is a small action that will have a big impact. Taking the time every day to think about what you are happy about and grateful for has a really positive impact on your outlook. Practicing gratitude improves your satisfaction with life and your well-being.

The things you acknowledge each day don't have to be huge, monumental life-changing things. There is as much value—maybe more—in the mundane, everyday things.

Imperfection Alert: The last thing I do at night when I shut my eyes to go to sleep is to think of three things that day that I am thankful for. Sometimes they can be very tiny things, sometimes bigger. It really doesn't matter. The important thing is to recognise positive things in your life. So it could be …

"I am thankful for getting to spend the day with my children at the park. I am grateful to the woman that let me go ahead of her in the supermarket queue when I was only buying bread and milk. I am thankful for the nice dinner we had this evening."

You see? There are no huge lottery winning items here in my life. Just everyday things that otherwise could pass me by. But by recognising them, and feeling thankful for them, we bring a positive outlook to our lives.

Imperfection Tip: It is said to be even more powerful if you write the three things down every day. I don't but only because I haven't got organised enough to do that. I think that however you do it, like anything, it is better to do it imperfectly than not at all. So if you can't write it down, that's ok. If you a miss a day, that's ok too. Just do what you can do and aspire to do better when you are able.

You can buy special gratitude journals. They look pretty and they often have inspiring quotes within them to aid you with your gratitude mindset. And if you want to invest, if it makes it a special thing for you to do, then by all means buy one. But if all you have is a scrappy piece of paper next to the bed and one of those mini-pencils that you took from Ikea, that will do the job too. You do you, but just make sure that you do something.

Imperfection Ideas:

\# Begin tonight. When you get in to bed think of three things you are grateful for.

\# Start a gratitude journal. Keep it by your bed with a pen so you can write in it every night.

Be disciplined – stick to three things only and use the ones that first come to mind, don't rationalise them.

Breathwork

Wow wow wow! Just wow! I am new to breathwork and honestly, it has CHANGED MY LIFE! See those upper-case letters there? THAT is how much breathwork has impacted my life for the better. Just try it and see for yourself.

Breathwork is an active practice that uses conscious breathing techniques to release memories and old patterns that may be holding you back. *Breath* in Latin means "spirit," and breathwork practice really does access and work on this level. It is an extremely healing practice, and endorphins are released during a session, which help you to feel good. Regular practice helps rewire your brain and realign your mind, body, and spirit. My breathwork practitioner, Jay Bradley, calls it "Spiritual CrossFit"!

Imperfection Tip: Set aside an hour a week to do a breathwork session. It could change your life.

The way a breathwork session works—or the ones I have done—is you lie down (a blanket is a good idea as you may get cool as your body relaxes. You need to be somewhere you will not be disturbed. An eye mask is a good idea too) and you are guided through the session while all the time working on the specific breath pattern. Depending on your class and practitioner, the breath pattern may vary—a three-part circular breath is what I do, but there are other techniques you might follow.

Focused breathing activates the parasympathetic nervous system, which is responsible for your body's well-being. Breathing in this special way means you take a lot more oxygen into your body than usual and, as oxygen flushes through you, during the session you will release endorphins and oxytocin.

Through the sessions I attend, we work through specific memories, as well as ancestral ties that may be holding you back. Releasing these old emotions shifts your energy to allow you to feel more present, more compassion, and more love in your life. People report lessened anxiety, less physical pain, and reduced stress. Breathwork is also reported to help digestion, boost immunity, lower cortisol, and lower blood pressure.

Imperfection Tip: Be ready for tetany during your breathwork session. Tetany describes the effect that you might experience whereby your hands can go claw-like and rigid (I get this). This is the effect of excess carbon dioxide. You may also feel tingling through your hands, feet, and mouth. I actually feel a tingling and tightening just above my knees weirdly. During the session, you may also experience light headedness, dry mouth, excess yawning (I get this one for the first five minutes), and you may feel very hot and/or very cold (I get cold). As with all exercise and practices, there are a whole list of contraindications for people that should avoid or be careful practicing breathwork, so make sure you let your practitioner know of any pre-existing conditions before you start.

<u>Imperfection Ideas</u>:

Find out where your nearest breathwork classes are.

Try a breathwork session – online or in person – this week.

Download an online breathwork session and commit to using it once a week. Set the time aside in your diary.

Charting Your Menstrual Cycle

If you menstruate or live with someone that menstruates, then having awareness of the changes that occur throughout the menstrual cycle and harnessing the ebbs and flows of this natural cycle will be beneficial to everyone within your household.

Where are you right now in your menstrual cycle? Do you know? And how do you feel at different points during your cycle? You may be aware of PMS-like symptoms and the feelings of rage that can occur around the time of bleeding.

But what about the rest of the cycle? The menstrual cycle is rather like the seasons in nature. The body, with every menstrual cycle, goes through spring, summer, autumn, and winter. And the body's energy levels alter as you go.

Winter is the time when you are bleeding. The body naturally wants to rest and be quiet. Spring comes and you start feeling more alert and your energy levels building. Summer is ovulation, and the body feels energised and alive. And then through to autumn where the body's energy levels start to drop back down and you slow up in preparation for the coming winter.

Without charting, chances are you might not have actively noticed the whole cycle of this natural rhythm. Our modern lives are not set up for us to stop and take note of these changes. One day is much the same as the next; we are online, available, whatever the day, whatever the weather. But what if you started to note each day of your cycle and how you are feeling? Perhaps you'll start to see a pattern.

Imperfection Tip: Beware of menstrual shame. Our culture does not honour the menstrual cycle. In fact, our culture does the opposite. There is negativity surrounding periods, there is an expectation that life continues irrespective of whatever point you are within your cycle. There is shame to admit to needing time off or to slow up because of period pains for example. It is seen as a weakness to admit to having difficulties or needing extra help through parts of your cycle. Even in advertisements, red-coloured menstrual blood is not allowed to be shown! The shame runs deep within the messages we receive from a young age and the chances are you may have internalised these. This is a good opportunity to use ho'oponopono. Think through your memories of menstruating. What is your memory of your first period? How did you feel? Was it celebrated? Were you ashamed? How openly could you talk about your menstruation? Do you have embarrassing moments in your past linked to your period? Think through them all and work through them using the ho'oponopono mantra. Clearing these blocks will help you when you move on to think about your cycle and the impact it has on your current life.

Back to your present life—Is there a time of your cycle where you feel particularly lethargic or particularly sociable? How could you work this in with your daily life to honour your natural energy levels? Could you set aside downtime where you don't have to be first in command of the household during the first day or two of menstruation? Or if that isn't feasible, what self-care could you work in for yourself on those days? Even just a ten-minute quiet time with a hot drink and your favourite chocolate? And how can you harness your more energetic times within your cycle?

Imperfection Alert: I have been charting consistently for about three years now. It has really given me insight to how I am feeling at certain points of the month due to my menstrual cycle. For example, usually I have a really good connection with my children but occasionally I just want to explode! Proper anger will bubble and I may end up shouting. But what I have noticed is that those times when I feel particularly frustrated and unheard are usually the day or two before my period. And so now when I feel like that, I know what's happening and I can be more mindful and put boundaries in place. That's not to say I never get cross, but it happens less regularly, and when I do, I can at least recognise what is happening and try to take some time for myself to honour those feelings.

Charting has opened my eyes not only to the negative feelings I can feel around my cycle, but also that I experience an amazing natural high in the middle of my cycle. For me, I get this high point around ovulation (approximately day 14), and I feel unstoppable. My energy levels are high, I feel so much love for my family and everyone around me, I feel like I can take on anything and I can change the world! It's a beautiful feeling and one I now know when to expect through charting. I can maximise its impact by working on my books more during that time, by being more visible online, by brainstorming new ideas, and by socialising more.

I love that crazy mid-cycle week I get, but actually I love it all. I love the snuggly, cuddly me-time of autumn and winter too. Once you begin to see the seasons within you and you start to honour them, it is such a privilege. You will feel more in touch with yourself and your life will benefit.

Summary of the Seasons:

- **Winter**—the time of bleeding. A time for quiet contemplation. Introversion. Reflect and review. Set intentions. Tune in to your instincts. Honour this time. (If you can take time out now, you will reap the benefits through the remainder of your month.)

- **Spring**—delicate but growing into your full self. Protect your energy at this time, don't be afraid to hold boundaries, to say no if you need to. Cherish and love yourself. Start to put plans into motion. (This is a great time for content planning if that's relevant.)

- **Summer**—you have bloomed. You are at full power. You are open, sociable, embracing all that you are. High energy. High resilience. Creativity is heightened. (This is a good time for networking, creating video content, for generally being more visible.)

- **Autumn**—you are shedding and releasing. You are stripping back. Cleaning, cleansing, nesting. Let go of what no longer serves you. Your inner critic can flair up at this time—this is your ego talking, which I like to think of like the scared child version of me. Be kind to your inner critic, take time to find out what it needs to feel safe. Protect and love yourself. (This is a good time for prioritising and getting things done before the winter season kicks in.)

Imperfection Tip: Start noting the day of your cycle you are on (if you don't know then wait until you next menstruate and mark that as day one) and jot down a couple of feelings every day. Can you see any patterns emerging? What could you build into your life to honour the natural energy from your cycle?

If you don't menstruate or you are taking contraceptives or medicines that mask your cycle, you can still benefit from charting. Did you know that menstruation often happens in sync with the moon? People will typically bleed on the new moon and ovulate on the full moon (called a white moon cycle), or, less commonly, will bleed on the full moon and ovulate on the new moon (called a red moon cycle). If you do not menstruate, you can chart instead directly to the moon's pattern. So begin on the new moon as day one and start to note how you feel, your emotions, your energy levels. And chart it through each day through the full moon and back to day one on the next new moon. It is likely that you will feel most energy around the full moon and in need of more time alone during the new moon, but keep an eye on what you are feeling as you may follow the less common red moon cycle pattern. Once you understand the natural ebb and flow of your own cycle, you can work that to your advantage and do more creative, sociable, and visible work during your times of high energy and work on quieter projects and build in more rest and reflection during your low-ebb times.

Imperfection Tip: During your winter period, find activities that will increase your oxytocin levels—your love hormone. Spending time with your children, self-care practices such as breathwork, yoga, meditation, listening to music, or having a massage will all help boost your oxytocin levels during this time (and most of them will help tone your vagus nerve too while you are at it).

Imperfection Ideas:

Think about how you could record your cycle – you could use a journal, an online app or just the notes on your phone. What is easiest and would work best for you?

When you start your bleed, record that as day one and make a few notes every day through your entire cycle back to day one again.

If you do not bleed, research when the next new moon is where you live and start recording from that day. Set yourself a reminder so you don't forget!

Social Media

Remove yourself from all social media immediately; it is the root of all evil and will ruin your life. Just kidding! We all know social media can be a drain on our lives; it isn't great for our mental health and it saps our time and energy levels. BUT. If we know how, and if we are more mindful, we can also use it to our advantage. So I don't say get rid of it (though a day a week social media free would do you the world of good). What I do recommend though, is to use it more mindfully.

First of all, recognise how long you spend on different sites. Most smartphones now have a usage monitor. I warn you, be prepared to assume your phone has it completely wrong as there is no way you spend THAT long on Twitter, is there?!?

If you are uncomfortable with the reality of the hours you are spending on these apps, then set some time limits on your phone so it turns off the app after a certain amount of time, or during certain hours of the day. Or even better, do a combination of the two.

If you know that you only have a certain amount of time on an app, it prevents the mindless scrolling that we can all fall foul of at times. I am sure most of us have popped on our phones before to quickly check something and found ourselves half an hour later scrolling down the feed page with a numb mind but somehow unable to switch off from the scrolling.

Imperfection Tip: If you limit your time on high-usage apps then the "mind-numb-scroll" is less likely to happen.

And then, secondly, be mindful about what you are looking at. Fill your feed with stuff that fills your cup. On Facebook, for example, you can unfollow people without having to unfriend them—so if your feed is getting clogged up with images of an old school friend that you haven't seen for fifteen years, you could unfollow them. They won't know, and you won't be bombarded any longer with images of the perfect life they are portraying (and that are maybe starting to get you down about your own seemingly less-perfect life). Use social media to connect with things that interest you and inspire you. Use it as a way to expand your mind and to gain knowledge about things you want to know more about. Feed your mind.

Imperfection Alert: I was spending more than six hours on my smartphone apps every day. I use my smartphone for work as well as leisure, but even so, I still can't believe that's true. Six hours?!? It wasn't like I was on it ALL the time. Just popping on here and there, reading a little bit of this, a little bit of that. Yet somehow it added up to SIX HOURS!! Seriously. I was shocked when I realised. And ashamed. How on earth did I even have six hours spare to do that? So I did what I advise here. I have a screen lock, which is activated for four hours during each day. I have a time limit on each of my most used apps. I make sure I have days where I don't use my phone for any social media. And when I'm on holiday, I rarely look at my phone at all. I have also rationed my feed so I see things that are more meaningful when I do log on—I love my Instagram feed now, it's almost like a self-help book and a big hug all at the same time.

Imperfection Tip: Your first step is to check your usage. How do you feel about it? How is it impacting on your life? What are you spending your time doing during those hours of usage? Are you filling your cup or numbing your mind? Be completely honest with yourself, and then think about what changes you could make to alter your habits. What limits could you put in place? And what could you delete from your feed, or add to your feed, to make sure that the content you are taking in is lifting you up?

<u>Imperfection Ideas</u>:

\# Check what your current usage is. How do you feel about it?

\# Don't use your phone for the first hour when you wake up, and the last hour before you go to bed.

\# Set screen downtimes and app limits to help reduce your current usage and habits.

\# Rationalise your apps so what you see on your feed is filling your cup.

Time in Nature

So simple but so important. We were made for living in nature. We are part of nature. IN nature is where we should be. All day, every day. But we aren't. The reality is that a typical day for many may look more like this:

- We leave our comfortable but sterile house in the morning,

- we drive around in our convenient but sterile metal box of a car,
- we sit all day in our soulless, air-conditioned office,
- we visit the gym on our way home, maybe spend a bit of time on the treadmill or swimming lengths in the pool,
- and then we go back to our comfortable but sterile house to go to bed.

Much of the air we have been breathing throughout the day has been recycled, air-con air. We have glimpsed the outside through the windows, but, in reality, we have spent almost zero time there. And this disconnect from nature day in, day out, is not good for us.

Let me ask you a question. When was the last time your bare feet touched the earth?

The earth has its own natural electrical charge, and this charge is beneficial to our human bodies. The way we live our lives means we have become disconnected from this energy; even our shoes with their rubber soles act as a barrier to this electrical charge.

"Grounding" is the term used to describe spending time bare foot, connecting with the earth. There are lots of studies out there that will show the amazing healing effects that spending time grounding can have on various illnesses. You can research in more detail if you are interested, or perhaps you are sceptical and that's ok too. But what harm can it do, to spend a bit of time each day or each week in bare feet? Lie on the ground or walk in bare foot for a while. See how it feels.

Imperfection Tip: Spend as much time as you can in nature. How can you get your "nature fix" each day? Can you spend your lunchtime away from your desk, outside in the park? Could you walk to work or get off the tube a station earlier to get a slightly longer walk outside? Could you fit in a walk after dinner? How about eating dinner outside in the garden?

Grounding aside, generally spending time in nature is something you should be aiming for. The seasons pass, and with our busy lives we let them slip by, often only noticing to grumble about how rainy it's been (I'm in the UK, we like to moan about the rain) or how cold it has been (we like to moan about this too), or how hot it is (this is our favourite, though we don't get to do this one very often).

But we are not usually stopping to notice the small changes—the first buds that push through the soil in spring, or to watch as the pale pink blossom on the trees dies off and starts to turn to fruit, or the difference in bird calls at different times of the year. Whether you live in the countryside or the city, you can find even the smallest patch to observe and notice the changes of the seasons. I have read that time in nature can reduce heart disease, diabetes, stress, and premature death. I don't know about the science specifically but I do know that time in nature feels good. If I am having a rough day or am feeling frustrated, just stepping outside the backdoor onto the grass and taking some deep breaths will make me feel better.

Imperfection Alert: Yesterday evening I felt really disconnected. We had been out all day, I was tired, and I was feeling frustrated that the kids kept bothering me and I wanted (needed) some down time (Note: I am in autumn, coming in to winter, in my menstrual cycle.). So I took myself off for a walk to our local nature reserve just around the corner from my house. At first my mind was racing with competing thoughts, but as I walked and looked and just breathed, my brain started to slow, the thoughts subsided and I could hear the birds, I could appreciate the amazing views, and I could appreciate all the flowers, berries, and trees. I was back home again in less than twenty minutes feeling like a new person. Time in nature is healing.

When we are outside experiencing nature, feeling the energy of the earth, looking and listening, our minds become stilled from the constant chatter. It is good for our soul, and we need to do more of it. The more we can reconnect with nature, the better.

Imperfection Ideas:

\# Commit to spending five minutes outside every day this week.

\# Go for one long walk every weekend for a month.

\# Take your shoes off right now and go and stand outside on a patch of grass (or anywhere outside if you don't have grass). Close your eyes and take ten deep, slow breaths.

Cold Showers

Cold showers are good for our bodies and our minds. They help make you more alert, they help your body to reduce stress levels, they increase the amount of white blood cells in your body so helping you to fight off infections more effectively, and they can help strengthen your will power (not least because standing in cold water is not an easy thing to do!). Well, at first it isn't easy, but it really does get easier. Most importantly, cold showers help stimulate the vagus nerve.

Imperfection Tip: Have your shower as usual and then at the very end turn down the water temperature as far down as it will go. At first you may only be able to tolerate a few brief seconds, but in time you will find your body builds up a tolerance and you'll quickly be able to withstand a couple of minutes or more.

Imperfection Alert: I love nothing more than a relaxing hot shower, so turning the dial down to cold wasn't something I relished. But, actually, once you get used to it, it is really an enjoyable thing to do. Not to sound crazy, but I now look forward to the cold-water blast for a few minutes at the end of my daily shower. While I am in there I also take time to do 100 cold water splashes on my face to refresh my skin and tighten my pores.

Imperfection Ideas:

Next time you shower, turn the dial down at the end of your shower just for a couple of seconds. Can you relax your body when it wants to tense up from the initial shock?

Set a timer and see if you can do thirty seconds under the cold water. Next time can you do a minute? Increase the time until you feel you are getting the maximum benefit.

Commit to finishing a shower with cold water every other day for a month.

Dancing

Dancing of course has a cardiovascular benefit, as with any exercise that raises your heart rate, and releases endorphins, which will make you feel good. But did you know that dancing has added benefits for your brain? A study conducted over 21 years and published in the New England Journal of Medicine looked at the impact of different activities on mental acuity on people aged over 75. The study found that while most physical activities did not have any effect at all, frequent dancing had a most significant effect on dementia rates. The reason for this is that dancing helps rewire the brain and helps with neuroplasticity (the brain's ability to form new pathways and connections).

Dancing also releases dopamine and serotonin into your body. It is going to make you feel good and reconnected. Dancing doesn't have to be a formal activity in the form of a dance class following set steps, though this is extra good for neuroplasticity, you'll also gain benefit from expressive dancing or just free-form dancing around your kitchen. The mental benefit comes when you get lost within what you are doing to the exclusion of other thoughts. When you can get into this flow then you'll be rewarded with similar benefits for your mind and body to when you meditate. So pop on some music and get dancing!

Imperfection Ideas:

Look in to dance classes local to you. What style of dance is available? Do any appeal?

Sign up for a trial class. Most dance teachers will offer a free lesson before you need to sign up.

Turn the music up when you are cooking dinner and have a dance by yourself in the kitchen.

Investigate if there are any online dance classes that you could follow.

Singing and Humming

This is another one that is good for the vagus nerve. The vagus nerve is connected to the back of your throat, so when you sing or hum, you stimulate the nerve and in doing so you activate the parasympathetic nervous system, which calms and relaxes you. On the flip-side, ever wondered why your voice wavers when you feel under threat? That would be your vagus nerve responding! By singing and humming, you can use your voice to directly tone the nerve.

In addition, singing and humming helps you to regulate your breathing, which also tones your vagus nerve. Ever been to or seen yoga classes where they all sit cross legged and emit an "omm" type of hum. This is why! Humming and singing releases endorphins and oxytocin, increases lymphatic circulation, reduces stress levels (cortisol), lowers blood pressure, and makes us feel calm. It has also been shown to boost the Immunoglobin A antibody.

Imperfection Tip: As a mood booster, make a playlist of songs that evoke happy memories and lift you up. When you play it and sing along, you will instantly reduce tension, increase energy, and feel happier.

To gain even more benefit from singing or humming, consider joining a singing group or choir. The benefits that you reap from singing and humming are boosted if you do it as part of a group, and you gain additional benefits too. Singing as part of a group helps forge social bonds and broadens social networks. The community aspect that a singing group provides is central to our well-being as humans. We are sociable creatures and we feel a sense of well-being when we feel connected to others.

In addition, similar to the benefit of learning formal dancing steps, the brain is stimulated by the work involved in remembering song words and learning new songs. Regular practice aids memory function, and for this reason, singing is an activity that can bring benefits for dementia patients.

It saddens me that we have become so removed from our musical roots on a personal and societal level. Music is found in every human culture on earth; our ancestors engaged in the communal practice of singing, and yet, in today's modern culture, singing has somehow become an elite activity for those that are "good at singing." But we are all good at singing. Or, should I say, we are all good enough. Singing is for everyone and it really pleases me to see the recent rise of community choirs and groups that are open to everyone without audition, regardless of singing ability. The power of social singing is being recognised once again, and as individuals and as a community, we will reap the benefits.

Imperfection Ideas:

Next time you are driving, turn the music up and sing as loudly and freely as you can.

\# Find out where your nearest choir or singing group is.

\# If you don't feel comfortable singing out loud, start with humming along to your favourite songs while at home.

Intermittent Fasting

Before we start, please understand that intermittent fasting is not dieting. I really don't like "diets." They don't work. If they did then they wouldn't keep inventing new ones. Intermittent fasting can bring about weight loss, but it brings a whole host of other benefits, and it is for those benefits I do it. The weight loss is more a by-product.

Digestion is an energy intensive process for your body. Fasting—allowing your body a block of time without needing to digest—stimulates the parasympathetic nervous system. By taking a rest from digestion, energy can be used instead for rebuilding the nervous system. We all do some level of fasting just through sleeping every night (assuming you are not raiding the fridge for snacks through the night). But ideally we should give our bodies a bit longer than this to reap the benefits of fasting. There are different types of intermittent fasting. Time-restricted fasting, which is what I'll talk about here, is the daily cyclical pattern of eating within set hours of the day and fasting for the remainder of them.

Giving your body rest from digestion is important. While in a fasting state, your body will burn body fat for energy. Fasting improves your insulin sensitivity to lower insulin and promote fat mobilisation, rather than relying on glucose to burn. Regular time-restricted fasting has been shown to lower LDL cholesterol (the "bad" kind), lower blood pressure, and lower insulin levels.

Imperfection Tip: Calculate how many hours you currently fast for (i.e., the period of time from when you finish your last bite of food before bed to when you have your first food the following day). Start with extending that period of time by an hour. So finish your last food an hour earlier, or start your first food of the day one hour later. And then build up from there, adding an hour on as you feel able. Following this process, I quickly got up to 16-18 hour fasts without a problem.

Note: When you are fasting, not only should you not eat, you shouldn't drink anything other than water, green/herbal teas, or black tea or coffee.

Imperfection Alert: I fast at the wrong time of day. I fast overnight and through the morning. Ideally one would eat earlier in the day and fast during the afternoon and overnight. However, fasting even at the "wrong time" of day still brings all the benefits we spoke about. It's just I could be helping myself even more if I fasted at the end of the day rather than at the beginning. The sticking point for me is our family meals. As a family, we sit and enjoy our evening meal together every night—we have arranged our work and lives to facilitate this as I feel it is really beneficial to us all to eat together as a family every day. This is our time when we have our most crazy conversations, when none of us are distracted by anything else, and I think it encourages healthier eating practices too. And so, if I changed my fasting hours, it would impact on this time, and currently I am prioritising our family meal time instead as that's more important to me. As I say throughout the book, we are not always aiming to achieve perfection, and this is a good example of where I am consciously being imperfect as that is what fits with my life. For now, it's the best I can do, and that is good enough.

Imperfection Ideas:

\# Calculate how long you are naturally fasting for at the moment i.e. the time from when you eat food on one day, to when you start eating the next. So if you ate dinner at 7pm, and then had a couple of chocolates at 9pm, 9pm would be your finishing time.

\# Try increasing your fasting window by half an hour, increasing to one hour over a period of three days.

\# Trial intermittent fasting for two weeks. How easily does it become part of your routine? How does your body feel?

- - Summary - -

I think in our culture we often ignore the holistic side of our lives, preferring to focus on the practicalities of the here and now. But if you can dig deeper and set aside time to care for yourself, you will come to realise the huge power of the changes we have discussed in this section. Caring for not only your body but also your mind will benefit every area of your life, and I urge you to commit to making a change today. Whether you start with improving the content of your social media feed and committing to reducing the mind-numb-scroll; or you might start a daily gratitude practice or journaling; or perhaps you could build some HIIT exercise or yoga in to your day. Remember, it is all about the small steps. And that first step you take will start your journey towards a better, more natural life.

CONCLUSION

Are you ready to make some changes? My hope by this point in the book is that your head is buzzing with ideas of what you want to change in your life. I find making positive changes within my life so exciting, and I hope you will feel the same as you start your own journey.

Remember, you are not aiming for perfection, you are just aiming to make a start. And I hope I have inspired you to take that step.

Imperfection Alert: I can't go without just one more Imperfection Alert! Before I make any change, I seem to have to argue with myself. My heart will start saying something like "I really think we should do some yoga every day, it'll be really good for us." And then my head will argue, "We just don't have the time for that! Our routine is set for the mornings, it works, it isn't feasible to find the extra time for this." And when I have thoughts like this, I just sit with them for a while. I don't fight the thoughts or try to rationalise it through. I just sit with the awareness of the conflict I am experiencing. And then eventually something will click, and I think, "I'll just give it a go and see what happens." And then I implement whatever it is—in this case, yoga—and it becomes just part of my routine and I look back and wonder why I ever thought it wasn't workable! But it seems I have to go through that period of conflict and awareness first. Every time. With some changes, the period of conflict may pass very quickly (for drinking more water, or for changing washing powder), and for others it can take a long time (to make the decision to stop drinking alcohol took me years).

But it is all a journey. And you need to honour the journey you are on. Don't worry about what anyone else is doing. Yes, be inspired by people and take their lessons, but don't compare yourself and find yourself lacking. Everyone's journey is unique to them and you can also never know the whole truth of anyone else's journey, so don't get caught up in comparisons.

What I hope this book will do is inspire you and encourage you to try something and see where it takes you. When I look back at how my life is now compared to even just the last two years, I would never have imagined I would be where I am today. And it all started with small, easy steps.

For more ideas and for inspiration throughout your week, follow me on Instagram and Facebook at iamsimplenaturallife.

Namaste.

ACKNOWLEDGMENTS

I want to thank Alex, my husband, for encouraging me to turn this book from an idea into a reality. I am grateful for his practical help supporting me and enabling me to find the time to actually write it.

I want to thank my daughters Enid, Emily, Alice, and Florence for providing me with the inspiration to be a better person, and in driving a desire within me to show them that you can make your dreams come true if you are brave enough to just take that first step.

Finally, I would like to thank my good friend Steph Heald for coaching me and providing the grounding, prompts, and reassurance I needed throughout this process.

ABOUT THE AUTHOR

Sarah is a mum of four and a writer from the UK. She has been writing professionally for twenty years, and she has a passion for finding ways to re-align our modern lifestyles with the natural world that we are innately part of.

Thank you for reading my book!

I really appreciate all of your feedback, and I love hearing what you have to say.

I need your input to make the next version of this book and my future books even better.

Please leave me an honest review on Amazon letting me know what you thought of the book.

Also find me by searching "I am simple natural life" on Facebook and "i_am_simple_natural_life" on Instagram for more ideas and updates.

Thanks so much!

Sarah Brooks

PS. And don't forget to download your FREE Kickstarter to help you start your journey today!
https://www.subscribepage.com/iamsimplenaturallifekickstarter